Beyond Celts, Germans and Scythians

**Duckworth Debates in Archaeology**

Series editor: Richard Hodges

**Published**

*Debating the Archaeological Heritage*
Robin Skeates

*Towns and Trade in the Age of Charlemagne*
Richard Hodges

*Loot, Legitimacy and Ownership*
Colin Renfrew

*Beyond Celts, Germans and Scythians*
Peter S. Wells

*Archaeology and Text*
John Moreland

**Forthcoming**

*The Origins of the English*
Catherine Hills

*Early Islamic Syria*
Alan Walmsley

# Beyond Celts, Germans and Scythians

## Archaeology and Identity in Iron Age Europe

Peter S. Wells

Duckworth

First published in 2001 by
Gerald Duckworth & Co. Ltd.
61 Frith Street, London W1D 3JL
Tel: 020 7434 4242
Fax: 020 7434 4420
Email: enquiries@duckworth-publishers.co.uk
www.ducknet.co.uk



A catalogue record for this book is available from the British Library

ISBN 0 7156 3036 9

Typeset by Ray Davies
Printed in Great Britain by
Bookcraft (Bath) Ltd, Bath, Avon

# Contents

# Preface

When most people think about the past, they want to know who built the mounds and hilltop fortresses that we see on the modern landscape, and who made the pottery, bronze ornaments and iron tools that farmers plough up in their fields and that archaeologists recover through excavation. They want to associate past human action with names that are familiar, to link the objects with humanity. Among the questions visitors to my excavations in southern Germany asked most often was, were they Celts or Germans?

Such attempts to identify peoples of prehistoric Europe depend upon names and descriptions in writings of Greek and Roman authors between the sixth century BC and the first century AD. Until recently, most archaeologists and historians accepted these characterizations by outside observers and interpreted the archaeology of the prehistoric Europeans in the context of those written accounts. But perspectives are changing. Many archaeologists now believe that it is important to try to understand how people identified themselves rather than accepting identities imposed upon them by outsiders.

In this book, I explore some of the ways that Iron Age Europeans created, transformed and expressed their identities, as we can discern the results of their actions in the archaeological evidence. Since the pioneering work of Fredrik Barth in the 1960s, we understand identity not as a static, inherent quality, but as a dynamic and contingent aspect of peoples' being. People create their identities in relation to their interactions with others. We must approach questions of identity in Iron Age Europe in the context of changes people experienced in the social world in which they lived.

The subject of identity is complex, and the quantity of often high-quality archaeological data from Iron Age Europe is vast. In this short book my aim is to present to the reader what I believe to be some of the central issues regarding identity in the Iron Age. Europe is the best-documented part of the world archaeologically, and in order to focus my presentation, I concentrate on the central regions of the continent – from France to Slovakia, from the Alps to the North European Plain – but I bring related developments elsewhere into the discussion.

It will be useful at the outset to state the principal points that I develop in the chapters that follow. Relevant literature is cited in the Bibliographic Essay. Given the scope of this book, I cannot always explain my reasoning in detail; but I refer the reader to literature that develops the arguments.

Identity is not a fixed thing, but a process in a relationship. Identity is always in a state of flux, and it exists only in relation to an other. It changes, and its expression changes, as the relationship and the other change.

During the Iron Age in Europe, there was much more mobility than most studies suggest – more people were moving and more objects circulating. Iron Age studies have focused on 'trade' and especially on 'Mediterranean imports', but these phenomena are only parts of a much more widespread and complex pattern of interaction. Identity in the Iron Age needs to be viewed in the context of this mobility.

We need to understand objects of material culture not only in terms of the purposes for which they were made, but as materializations, or material expressions, of relations between individuals and groups. The 'meaning' of an object changes depending upon the significance assigned to it by people; it is not fixed by the circumstances of its manufacture.

Archaeological sites are static configurations of material culture that once played active roles in processes of interaction between people. The usual focus on the physical structure and spatial arrangement of material on archaeological sites can obscure our understanding of the processes of which the sites are the static representations of single moments in the actions of human agents.

Texts are cultural products. What Herodotus tells us about Scythians and Caesar says about Gaul are creations of those particular writers, based on their perceptions, the historical circumstances under which they were observing and writing, their purposes in communicating with their audiences and other culturally determined factors.

Like archaeological sites, texts are static representations of historically specific times in dynamic relationships. Peoples about whom texts are written change continuously, but texts often do not reflect such change.

People respond to representations of themselves. They are usually interested in learning about how they are understood and represented by outsiders, and their self-conceptions are affected by how they think others view them.

Chapter 1 reviews recent theoretical discussion about identity, and especially the study of identity through archaeological evidence, in order to explain my positions on the issues and to situate the book in past and present debates. The reader familiar with the ongoing discussion may wish to begin immediately with Chapter 2.

I have written this book principally for the student of European archaeology and early history, as well as for the interested general reader. It must be emphasized that it is a very brief and highly selective outline of an immensely large and complex topic. I hope that my efforts to synthesize and to suggest new ways of thinking about the archaeological evidence may also interest specialists in European archaeology and history.

# Acknowledgments

Many people have been generous in providing advice in answer to my questions and in sending books, offprints and photographs that have been valuable sources for this book. Richard Hodges of the University of East Anglia first suggested this project. Deborah Blake of Duckworth has provided excellent advice throughout the preparation process. David Anthony of Hartwick College, Oneonta NY, has discussed issues of identity with me at length and has given me many ideas. Others who have helped in a variety of ways are Joan Aruz, New York; Jörg Biel, Stuttgart; Rolf Dehn, Freiburg; Michael Dietler, Chicago; Timothy Dunnigan, Minneapolis; Berndt Engelhardt, Landshut; Otto-Herman Frey, Marburg; Jochen Haas, Stuttgart; Ulla Lund Hansen, Copenhagen; Fritz-Rudolf Herrmann, Wiesbaden; J.D. Hill, London; Hans-Eckart Joachim, Bonn; Rosemary Joyce, Berkeley; Greg Laden, Minneapolis; Oliver Nicholson, Minneapolis; Daniel Potts, Sydney; Karen Rubinson, New York; Frederick Suppe, Muncie IN; Ann Waltner, Minneapolis; David Wigg, Frankfurt; Willem Willems, Amersfoort; Werner Zanier, Munich. I thank my wife Joan and my sons Chris and Nick for their constant good-humoured support.

# List of Figures

# 1

# Identity and the Archaeology of the Iron Age

The issue of identity has been a major theme of anthropological research since the 1970s and in archaeology since the 1980s. In this first chapter, I outline some of the principal aspects of recent thinking that pertain most directly to our attempts to understand identity in Iron Age Europe. For background discussion and elaboration of these points, references in the Bibliographic Essay will lead the reader into the relevant literature.

## Approaching identity in a different world

### *Whose view of identity?*

Writing around the middle of the fifth century BC, the Greek author Herodotus (IV.49) informs us that the source of the Danube River lies in the lands of the Celts, who are among the most western of Europe's peoples. The same river, he notes, flows across the continent to the edge of the land of the Scythians, a nomadic people whose customs he describes in some detail. The Roman Julius Caesar, writing about four centuries after Herodotus, also speaks of Celts, who are, he says, the same as the people Romans know as Gauls (I.1). Caesar contrasts them with groups he calls Germans, who live east of the Rhine, while Celts live west of it. In many respects,

Germans are culturally less complex than Celts, and much more different from Romans.

Thus Iron Age peoples of Europe first become known to us as named groups, situated geographically and ascribed particular characteristics and behaviours by Greek and Roman writers. On the basis of such references in the textual sources, modern investigators draw maps that show the locations of different groups, situated in specific places in Europe. The effect of such maps is to suggest that the names designate clearly defined peoples, and that their locations show where they resided, implying that group boundaries were distinct and persistent.

Until a generation or two ago, these identities ascribed to indigenous peoples of Europe by Greek and Roman writers were generally accepted by the majority of archaeologists and historians as well as by the interested public. But now recent advances in anthropology, archaeology, historiography and Greek and Roman history have taught us that the situation is much more complex. We cannot simply accept assertions about the 'barbarian' peoples and their identities that come from Greek and Roman writers. We must approach the surviving texts not as statements of objective fact, but as culturally constituted representations. Our task is to develop critically-informed ways to understand what the texts can tell us – both about the Iron Age peoples and about the writers who described them. The growing body of scholarship on written accounts of non-literate indigenous peoples offers useful techniques for approaching the Greek and Roman texts.

My principal purpose here is not to critique interpretations of the Greek and Roman writings about the barbarians to the north. Rather, it is to focus on what the Iron Age Europeans can communicate to us through their material culture. As the only written sources of information about these Iron Age peoples, the Classical texts are important, and, interpreted critically in light of recent research on representation in imperial and colonial contexts, they can provide significant information. It is useful at the outset to distinguish between the three major sources of information about identity among Iron Age Europeans. The relationships between these sources are complex, and the differences are important.

First, information that peoples of Iron Age Europe present about themselves, through their material culture. They did not leave written texts that inform us about their identities, but they created, arranged and patterned a wide variety of material culture that can provide us with a wealth of information about ways that they understood, expressed and negotiated their identities.

Secondly, information that Greek and Roman authors provide about their northern neighbours in the form of texts that have been preserved. These documents are all outsiders' accounts and need to be evaluated with much greater critical thoughtfulness than has usually been practised. Examined in concert with the archaeological evidence, they can provide important supplementary information.

Thirdly, information created by modern investigators, on the basis of both the archaeology and the ancient texts. A great deal of accepted knowledge about the identity of the Iron Age Europeans is passed along in modern scholarly tradition without reference back to the original material culture created by the prehistoric peoples.

Much of the discussion in this chapter revolves around the importance of distinguishing between these three kinds of sources.

## *Identity and archaeology*

Archaeologists and historians have tended to treat the Greek and Roman texts that name and describe Iron Age Europeans largely as if they were objective descriptions by writers in modern Western society, such that we can accept the assertions matter-of-factly and immediately understand the reality they portray as part of our reality. Similarly, archaeological evidence from Iron Age Europe has generally been interpreted as if the people who created the materials were very much like us – as if they organized and lived their lives in ways similar to the way we do, and viewed their social, natural and supernatural surroundings as members of modern Western industrial societies do.

The social and spiritual world of Iron Age Europeans was probably very different from anything we know and from anything we can imagine. The lack of such basic modern necessities as electricity, telephones, motorized vehicles and antibiotics should make apparent that their world and the way they viewed it were very different from our experience. Vast changes in social organization, religious belief and understanding of nature have transformed our attitudes, beliefs and behaviours over the past 2000 years. The past is indeed foreign to us. Our challenge is to devise ways to examine that world and the people who lived in it without letting our preconceptions dominate our thinking. Archaeologists including John Barrett, Charlotte Fabech and J.D. Hill have made important contributions in this direction, demonstrating that Iron Age peoples behaved in ways that are fundamentally foreign to us.

To understand better how Iron Age peoples viewed the world in which they lived, we need to broaden our thinking beyond the standard categories that encompass the way we understand our own society. The categories that we create to investigate and discuss Iron Age peoples, such as 'economy', 'society', 'political systems' and 'religion'; and the way we think about the archaeological evidence in terms of 'settlements', 'cemeteries', 'ritual sites' and 'deposits' have been useful for developing a common archaeological discourse about the past. But they impose a structure on the evidence that is created in our minds and one that probably differs from those that were in the minds of the people we are studying. As Walter Pohl observes, even the very words we use to describe and discuss the past are problematic, since they belong to a different context from that of Iron Age Europe. Distinctions that we make between tools and ornaments, for example, may be different from the ways Iron Age people regarded their material culture. We must, of course, make do with the means of communication available to us. But keeping aware of the shortcomings of our concepts and vocabulary for capturing the essence of Iron Age life can help us to consider new interpretations of the evidence.

### *An archaeology of practice*

Most research that deals directly or indirectly with issues of identity in Iron Age Europe has focused on what we regard as specific types of objects, such as fibulae, pottery, coins and *oppidum* settlements, and on signs of distinction such as imported luxuries, objects made of valuable materials or unusually finely crafted products. Thus we read of a 'Celtic sword' or a 'Germanic fibula' or a 'Scythian arrowhead'. Such terminology is based on assumptions by modern investigators concerning what a particular style of fibula indicates about the group to which its wearer belonged, or what a painted Attic *kylix* tells about the status of a buried individual.

One means of approaching questions of identity that involves less of our own preconceptions and categorizations is to focus on what the people we are studying actually did – an archaeology of practice – rather than concentrating on types of objects and categories of wealth in graves. We can examine how they arranged their dwellings, how they formed and decorated their pottery, what ornaments they chose to make and wear, how they arranged goods in burial assemblages, deposited iron tools in pits and built rectangular enclosures. I use the word 'practice' in the sense of 'how people do things' without any of the political implications often associated with the term.

Our upbringing, education and everyday life teach us to focus attention, when communicating with others, on verbal expression. We are most conscious of what we and other people say. Our ever-increasing use of media that allow communication over distance, in which we do not see the person with whom we are interacting, intensifies this focus on the verbal. In the Iron Age, most interpersonal communication was face-to-face, and the non-verbal element played a much greater role in communication than it does for us today. Even now when interacting persons can see one another, non-verbal behaviours – gestures, body movements, smiles or frowns – play an important role in the communication of information. A person can say one thing, but indicate the opposite through non-verbal means.

In the expression of identity, non-verbal communication offers a broad medium of discourse separate from verbal communication. It can be argued that non-verbal media are much richer and more detailed, because they are not restricted to the limited number of words that people have available with which to communicate. Personal appearance, including varieties of hair style, facial cosmetics, beards and moustaches, tattoos and piercings, combinations of clothing and jewellery, suntans or lack thereof, are among non-verbal media that offer possibilities in which the individual can create and express identity. In the realm of action, the individual has at his/her disposal an infinite variety of facial expressions, postures, hand and head gestures, ways of shaking hands and styles of walking, to cite just a few examples.

Iron Age peoples of temperate Europe were for the most part non-literate. Jack Goody has shown that non-literate peoples think and behave in some ways that are fundamentally different from literate groups. In non-literate societies, memory plays a much greater role in the preservation of tradition. In literate societies, practice of different kinds – content of stories, structure and performance of ritual, rules that guide the building of houses and the laying out of settlements – is more standardized than in non-literate societies. Because of reliance on memory, practice in non-literate societies is more diverse. Stories vary in different retellings, according to storyteller and circumstances. Details in the performance of complex rituals vary for the same reason, as do practices for house-building and settlement organization. For this reason, neighbouring groups in non-literate societies often develop different practices to a much greater extent than those in literate societies. Material objects play crucial roles as mnemonic devices to help performers of rituals and tellers of stories remember sequences of actions.

### *Ethnicity and identity: the past in the present and the present in the past*

Identity is a prominent theme in the world today, and modern contexts demonstrate why specific historical circumstances make identity matter. Perceived and often politically encouraged differences between groups of people in Kosovo, Bosnia and Herzegovina; among the Hutu and Tutsi in Rwanda; among groups in Northern Ireland, Spain, Corsica, India, Pakistan, Sri Lanka and many other countries, fuel often savage violence. Less violent but no less real are strong feelings of group identity in Scotland, Wales, Belgium, Quebec and Hawaii. As European countries strive to combine resources and policies with the introduction of the euro, the opening of borders and the creation of common regulations, questions of national autonomy and immigration issues frequently become debates over identity. Identity issues play a major role in interactions between Native American communities and others in American society, and between different communities throughout North and South America. Any consideration of this topic in the past must take account of our present experiences and attitudes. We as investigators are shaped by the world we live in, and our present circumstances affect our thinking about the past. At the same time, what we learn about the past affects our understanding of, and our approaches to, the present.

The theme of identity is much discussed today in many academic disciplines, popular culture and political debate. The importance of this subject to modern discourse is readily apparent from book titles, papers in journals, newspaper and magazine articles and public disputes over educational policies.

The cultural and national identities of many modern European countries, and of groups who migrated from Europe to other parts of the world, are closely linked to the perceived identities of the inhabitants of Europe during the centuries before and after the Roman conquest, when indigenous peoples were first named and described by Classical authors. The Gauls of the Late Iron Age, personified by such figures as Vercingetorix, have played an important role in national identity in France. In Germany, perceived links with the ancient Germans described by Caesar and Tacitus were significant in the creation of national identity from the sixteenth to the nineteenth century, and were manipulated to horrific ends in the 1930s and early 1940s. Rembrandt's paintings of Civilis, leader of the Batavians in their rebellion against Rome, provide an early modern example of the linking of Dutch identity with Iron Age forebears, at a time of national struggle for independence from Spain. Today, as European nations work to forge economic, political and cultural unity, the question of the significance of identities linked with the distant past has particular resonance.

The idea of 'Celts' provides a good example of the multifarious uses to which perceptions of past identities are put. The Celts have been portrayed in recent years as a great force of unification in ancient Europe. In the preface to the catalogue of the major international exhibition in Venice in 1991, the organizers make explicit that the purpose of the event was to draw attention to and to celebrate this unifying people of early Europe. But, the reader asks, were the Celts really unifiers of Europe, or were the organizers of the exhibition creating that role for them? (The exhibition was held, not in a place now strongly associated with the idea of Celticness, such as Ireland, Wales or France, but in northern Italy.) Frequently the Iron Age of Europe is referred to as the 'Celtic' Iron Age, and the adjectives *celtique* and *keltisch* are often used in place of 'Iron Age'. In other contexts, 'Celt' means something very different. At the time of Caesar, 'Celt' was contrasted with 'German' to denote the peoples north of the Alps in western and central Europe. Today, 'Celtic' refers most frequently to peoples of Ireland, Wales and Brittany, where languages classified as Celtic have survived into modern times. Thus the name can mean many different things, depending on the context in which it is used.

### *Material culture, identity and agency*

Focusing on the subject of identity provides a way to understand much in the patterns of archaeological evidence that is not readily explicable in terms of the economic and social paradigms that have dominated research in the recent past. The people we are studying probably did not think of identity as a category of feeling and behaviour. What we call identity was embedded in the way they viewed their world, interacted with others and went about their everyday lives.

The basis of this relatively new approach in prehistoric archaeology lies in important changes in archaeology and related disciplines during the past few decades. For present purposes these can be summarized in terms of three trends. First, we understand material culture not just as the means by which humans interact with their natural and social environments, to produce food, build shelters, make clothing and conflict with neighbours. Objects that people make and use are also media of communication, transmitting information of different kinds from one individual to another and between groups. Thus the material evidence of archaeology can be understood in terms of the social interactions of which it was part. Secondly, recent research in cultural anthropology and history demonstrates that identity is not a fixed quality, but is fluid, dynamic and contingent. Individuals and groups can, and do, change their identities with circumstances. Third, in a variety of social science fields, including anthropology, archaeology and history, investigators focus increasingly on the role of individual agency in examining patterns of behaviour and change. In any context, individuals have some degree of choice in their actions. Approaching the material evidence of the past in terms of individual agency provides a useful tool for understanding variability in behaviour and expression.

### *Definitions and characteristics of identity*

Identity is the ever-changing feeling and knowledge people have about their similarity to and difference from others. The aspect of relation is critical – without an 'other' there can be no 'self'. All human action must be understood within a context of the individual's perception of the self's identity. In order for the individual to function as a member of any group – family, community, nation – he or she must have a sense of how he/she fits into the group and of how that group differs from others. Identity provides the individual with the knowledge of how to treat others in contexts of interaction.

Identity may be defined and examined on any level – the individual in relation to another individual, in relation to the family, to the neighbourhood, to the community, to the region, to the ethnicity or to the nation, to use some common categories. The greater the range of others in relation to whom the individual conceives his/her identity, the more complex and multi-faceted the individual's identity.

In the course of the twentieth century, changes have taken place in understanding the nature of identity. Earlier conceptions tended to view identity as natural and inherent – the individual was born into a specific identity and remained with that identity throughout life. Studies of the past few decades, on the other hand, emphasize a view that identity is more complex. It derives partly from upbringing, but is also constructed, fluid and dynamic; to a large extent, it is a creation of the individual that can change with circumstances.

Jones (1997: 84) defines ethnic groups as 'culturally ascribed identity groups, which are based on the expression of a real or assumed shared culture and common descent (usually through the objectification of cultural, linguistic, religious, historical and/or physical characteristics)'. Grahame (1998: 158) adds the caveat 'ethnicity must refer to the self-conscious identification that individuals have with a particular group and not to arbitrary distributions ... defined by an external observer'. Much discussion surrounds the question of how ethnic identity is created and expressed. One position, associated with the terms primordialist and essentialist, emphasizes ethnic identity as a feeling shared by people as the result of real or imagined common ancestors or common traditions and experiences. Another, known as the instrumentalist or social constructionist, views ethnicity more as a means to some kind of political, economic or social advantage. These perspectives need not be viewed in opposition, but can be understood as aspects of the same process, or as different ways for us as investigators to think about identity. David Anthony has cogently observed that the instrumentalist view of identity has developed largely on the basis of the study of migrant groups adapting to new circumstances. As Bentley suggests, we need to consider the creation and transformation of ethnic identity in terms of the whole panoply of social processes in which the individual and the group engage.

In a recent paper, Jones develops a useful approach to the problem through Bourdieu's concept of the *habitus*. We can understand identity as formed through the processes of interaction between the individual's (or group's) *habitus* – basic assumptions, beliefs and practices – and the larger social and political context of interaction with the cultural landscape. Thus a role is played both by internal factors that include upbringing, education, religion, family traditions and the practices of everyday life, and by external factors such as interactions with neighbouring villages, trade relations with distant groups and influences from expanding states. This approach allows for the contributions of many diverse factors that come together to create the complex phenomenon commonly called ethnic identity.

## Expressing identity

### *Behaviour and identity*

People express their identity as individuals, as members of families and communities, of corporate groups and of national or ethnic entities, through a wide range of different media and behaviours. Sometimes expression is conscious, as when we wave a flag, other times not; it is not always easy for the observer to determine whether the individuals involved were conscious of their expression of identity. The expressions include language and accent, personal appearance, dress, music, foods, food preparation and consumption, ritual (such as dance, feasts and religious ceremonies), house form, arrangement of internal space and styles of ornamentation. Many of these categories, such as language, music, dance and tattooing, are available for analysis by linguists, cultural anthropologists and other researchers concerned with living peoples, but usually not recoverable by archaeologists. For purposes of examining identity in the prehistoric Iron Age, we need to focus on expressions through material culture that may survive the passage of time. But as Pohl and others have noted, the relationship between these expressions and identity is complex and varied.

### *Material manifestations*

Recent studies show how objects that people make and use can be understood as media of social action and as such play roles in shaping relations between people. We cannot assume a recurrent, consistent correlation between a particular kind of material culture and a specific identity. For example, we cannot speak of a 'Celtic fibula' or a 'Germanic belt hook'. Context is all important. The same object can have different meanings in different situations, and similar meanings can be conveyed by different objects.

Personal ornamentation, including clothing and jewellery, is one medium for the expression of identity. Metal, glass and amber ornaments are abundant from Iron Age European contexts, and they vary widely in form and style. They thus offer a rich source of information about variability in material culture. Burials often provide good evidence about dress and ornaments, especially in the form of bronze and iron jewellery such as fibulae, belt attachments, pendants and rings. In burial contexts, we can associate particular assemblages of personal ornaments with specific individuals.

The character – form and decoration – of objects used in the course of everyday life can be another important indicator, as Dietler and Herbich show for pottery. Investigators working in Britain and in the Netherlands demonstrate how the form, orientation and layout of Iron Age houses were strong markers of identity, reflecting values and traditions of the persons who lived in them. This point is supported by the maintenance of the Iron Age-type house in the Netherlands as an expression of persistent local identity long after the Roman conquest of the region.

Some recent studies suggest that practices of everyday life and of ritual are among the most informative arenas of expression. As the result of upbringing and education, people in one society do things one way, those in another do them another way. The ways people prepare and consume meals, arrange furniture in their houses and assemble their garments for the day, all tell something about who they are. Material residues of everyday activities can provide valuable information about identities.

Ritual, including burial but also other events such as religious ceremonies, political festivals and seasonal feasts, is a category of human behaviour in which the deepest meanings and traditions of a society are expressed. Many ritual activities have significant material aspects, in which essential meanings and relationships in society are embodied in objects that can be susceptible to archaeological analysis. In the process of ritual, objects can become materializations of social relations and of values. Funerary ritual is particularly important for examining identity issues in the Iron Age, because it often leaves significant material remains. Much of the ceremony is not readily apparent to archaeologists, but graves constitute an important and potentially very informative part of the ritual. The ways in which the body was treated, the character of burial structures, the choice and position of grave goods and many other variables, can all inform us about identity. The grave as encountered by the archaeologist needs to be understood as the result of a series of materially expressed actions performed for specific social reasons.

For Iron Age Europe, most information about funerary rituals derives from burials alone. Yet early ethnohistoric accounts make clear that creating and outfitting a grave is only one aspect of mortuary practice. Herodotus' description of a royal Scythian funerary ceremony provides an instructive example, and archaeological excavations of burials in southern Ukraine show the material manifestations of those practices. It is important to note that the ceremony was a public event, involving many participant-observers from the community. The burial process can be understood as a series of social statements that remained in the memories of the participants and served to structure their ideas about their community and society and about their place in them. Recent excavations at Iron Age burial sites, such as Vix in France, the Glauberg in Germany and Filippovka in Russia, reveal important information that expands our understanding of mortuary ritual from the grave to the wider arena of the entire cemetery landscape.

### *Identifying others*

This book focuses on the ways Iron Age peoples of Europe constructed and expressed their identities. But since a major source of information about Iron Age Europeans comes to us through observations made by outsiders, we need to consider the problem of how outsiders perceive and express identities of peoples they encounter. Extensive research in recent decades on the subject of outsiders' accounts provides useful perspectives on the issues.

Outsiders' written accounts represent other peoples in categories created by the writers. Such observers often name peoples they encounter with designations of their own devising, and they distinguish groups and boundaries that often do not correspond to those perceived by the peoples themselves. Edward Said's *Orientalism* (1978), in which he shows how European conceptions and representations of the peoples of the Near East differed from the ways that those peoples perceived themselves, has been an important influence in research on these issues. Subsequent analyses of outsiders' representations of many other peoples provide a rich resource for developing approaches to the Greek and Latin texts concerning Iron Age Europeans.

Outside observers represent peoples not only through verbal description, but also through pictorial representation in media that include painting, sculpture and reliefs, for example on Roman coins. These forms of discourse can be even more influential than written accounts for members of the society that produced them, because they are more widely accessible than texts in societies in which literacy is limited. In the case of Iron Age Europe, Greek and Roman sculpture and coinage were visual media in which the Mediterranean societies represented peoples to their north. These representations require a critical approach similar to that applied to texts.

## Dynamics of identity

### *Change and identity*

The individual's sense of identity is a dynamic relationship that can be understood in terms of interaction between results of upbringing and life experience. Similarly, for other levels – family, community, ethnicity; however we want to think about group identity – the feeling of identity is a dynamic relationship between a past tradition and present interaction. Current understanding of these principles derives both from theoretical work and from observation of patterns in the modern world. Issues of identity become much more relevant to people's lives and larger in their consciousness during times of particularly active change.

Jones presents a good example of the process, based on fieldwork by Comaroff and Comaroff. The indigenous group of southern Africa known to us as the Tswana first developed a clear and well-defined sense of themselves as a distinct people in the process of interaction with European missionaries. Before the Europeans arrived on the scene, there had been no reason for these indigenous communities to create a self-conscious sense of themselves as a distinct people. Only with the change in their situation – the appearance of people with clearly different traditions, practices, language and material culture – were these people motivated to create an identity as a people – an ethnicity – crafted in opposition to what they saw as the characteristics of the Europeans. This identity was created on the basis of practices, traditions and material objects which had long been part of their way of life, but which attained potent new significance as they assumed the roles of identity markers.

### *How material culture structures identity*

People's relationship with their material culture is reflexive. They make, decorate, buy or wear objects in part in order to communicate particular information about themselves. At the same time, the process of making, decorating, buying, receiving and wearing objects plays a part in the shaping of that identity. We do not just use our material culture, we interact with it. This aspect of the relationship between people and objects has been explored in a variety of contexts, both ancient and modern, and involving both everyday objects of local origin and exotic imported goods. It is in the practice of daily life, in the course of which people make, purchase and use their material objects, that they create their identities, and the objects play essential roles in that process. As people use objects, the users, the meaning of the objects and the relationships between the people and the objects, all change. When people integrate foreign objects into their daily lives or ritual practices, those goods often play a special role in structuring their identities, as studies by

Thomas and Orlove demonstrate. In the process of interaction with the material world, people constantly renegotiate and restructure their identities.

### *Outsiders' texts and dynamics of identity*

The existence of texts written by members of complex literate societies that name and describe smaller-scale, non-literate peoples – such as the Greek and Roman accounts of the Iron Age Europeans – is a widespread phenomenon in time and space. In the ancient Near East, cuneiform texts represented neighbouring peoples to the literate societies of Mesopotamia in terms similar to those of the Greek and Roman writers. Strikingly similar kinds of representations are evident in other early literary traditions, such as in China and in Mesoamerica. From these early accounts, and from much more abundant later texts, particularly European accounts of interactions with indigenous peoples from the sixteenth to the nineteenth century, it is clear that there are important similarities in the ways that members of complex state societies regard smaller-scale societies with which they come into contact.

Several points emerge from these studies that will be important in the chapters that follow. When outsiders describe indigenous peoples, the categories they use are created by the outsiders – the observers generally do not attempt to reproduce categories of the peoples they describe. The descriptions of indigenous peoples are constructs, based to a large extent upon the outsiders' views of the world, but with some basis in the reality of the groups under examination. Outsiders typically do not understand the nature of change among peoples they observe. As Eric Wolf (1982) put it, from the perspective of the imperial writers, the indigenous peoples were 'without history' – they were static, never-changing. Neil Whitehead's study of Walter Raleigh's accounts of native peoples of northeastern

South America, analysed with archaeological and ethnohistorical sources of information, provides a good example. In this case, and in the majority of the Classical accounts of Iron Age Europeans, the imperial writers seem unaware of the impact of contact before the observations were made that form the basis of the textual accounts. By the time the observers composed their texts, the societies had already changed, in part as a result of their interactions with the imperial society.

Studies by cultural anthropologists working in the Americas demonstrate this important phenomenon in interactions between indigenous peoples and outsiders, in particular Spaniards and English. Jonathan Hill explains how the group known as the Caribes developed from the Aruacas in direct response to Spanish conquests. Albers and Hickerson show how new peoples with new identities formed on the Great Plains of North America as the result of changes set in motion by interaction with Europeans in the late nineteenth century. Much of this negotiation and formation of group identity was accompanied by migration, a phenomenon often linked to interaction with complex outside societies. These examples suggest mechanisms for us to consider as we examine evidence from Iron Age Europe preceding Caesar's campaigns in Gaul. In particular, they help us to understand why Caesar's descriptions take no account of the situation that the archaeology indicates before 100 BC (see Chapters 5 and 6).

### *The 'tribal zone'*

In their studies of interaction between indigenous peoples and incoming complex societies, Ferguson, Whitehead and Hill have developed the concept of the tribal zone. This is a sphere of interaction in which complex societies come into regular contact with less complex ones. Their argument, based upon a wide range of comparative studies in different parts of the world, is that what we know as 'tribes' – polities comprised of a few thousand people with a distinct territory and a specified leader – are largely creations of processes of interaction between expansionary state-level societies and indigenous ones. Indigenous, non-state societies typically have fluid territorial and political boundaries, only weakly developed political hierarchies and a less formalized sense of identity as a group. Intermarriage, movement between groups and fluid rather than rigid leadership structures typically characterize such societies before the arrival on the scene of complex states. The arrival of complex societies sets in motion a series of changes that result in 'tribalization' – the creation of more self-consciously defined groups, with a sense of territory, group identity and a political structure focused on a single leader – 'king' or 'chief'. This model provides a useful way of understanding patterns of change in identity among Iron Age peoples in contact with Mediterranean societies.

### *Mobility, interaction and identity*

Geographically beyond the tribal zone, historical and ethnohistoric accounts demonstrate the long-distance effect of expanding complex societies on smaller indigenous communities. In cases where no written records document such long-distance effects, as in Iron Age Europe, imported goods, adapted styles and motifs and borrowed practices can serve as proxies through which we can examine change. In past studies of Mediterranean imports, the emphasis of research has been on using the imported objects for establishing chronologies, studying trade systems and exploring mechanisms such as prestige-good economies, centre-periphery interactions and borrowing of customs. New approaches suggest how we can understand imports in terms of the ways they were used for structuring identities among the peoples who acquired them. Rogers, Thomas and

Orlove document ways that imports play such roles in ethnographic contexts, and Hansen has shown how this approach helps us understand political change in Roman Iron Age Denmark. As Thomas emphasizes, the role and meaning of imports are not at all clear from their purpose in the society that created them; rather, we need to investigate the ways in which their recipients and consumers used them to create their own meanings. These meanings are often closely linked with the establishment of new identities related to the interactions in which the societies are engaged.

*

Presenting a thematic treatment of archaeological and historical information from a complex context such as Iron Age Europe requires compromise, and I outline here the structure that I have chosen for the following chapters. Chapter 2 examines evidence and context from the Early Iron Age, about 800-475 BC, Chapter 3 from the earlier part of the Late Iron Age (475-200 BC). Chapter 4 considers texts that pertain to the Iron Age to about 200 BC. Chapter 5 focuses on the later part of the Late Iron Age, 200 BC to the Roman conquest. Chapter 6 examines some of the Greek and Roman texts from this time of intensive interaction. In Chapter 7, I consider the complex issue of how Greek and Roman representations of Iron Age Europeans affected those peoples' ideas about their identities.

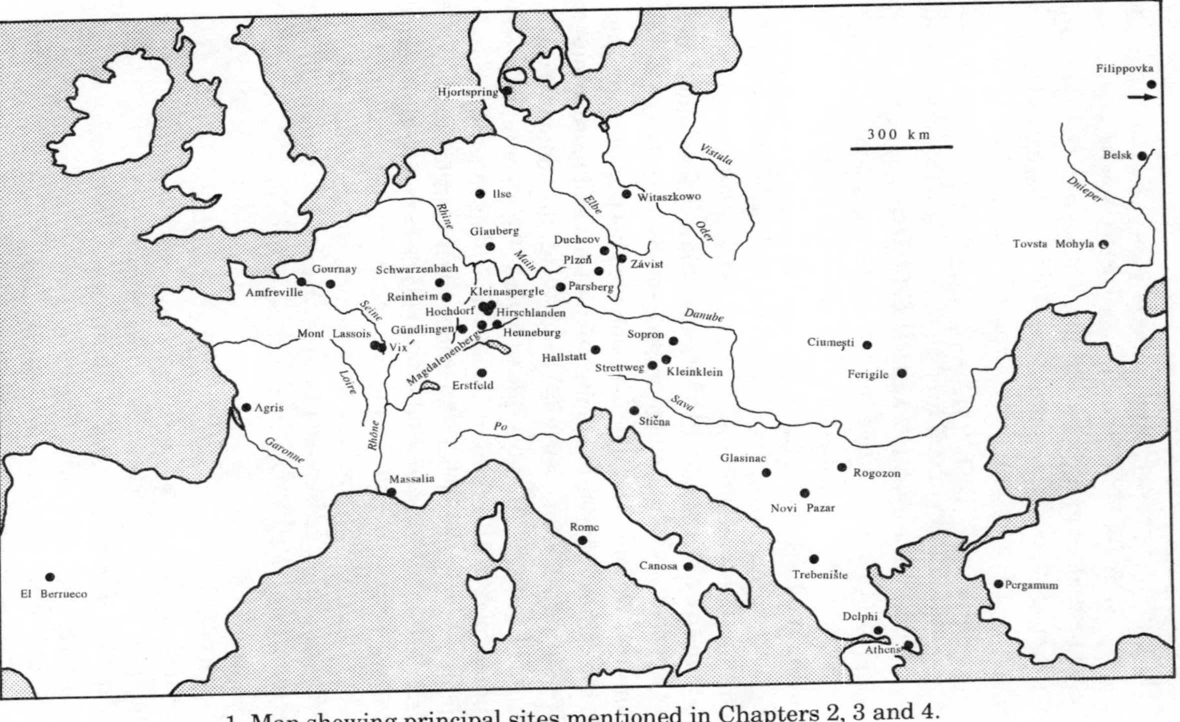

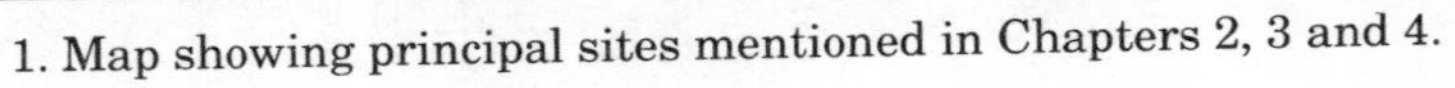
1. Map showing principal sites mentioned in Chapters 2, 3 and 4.

# 2

# Changing Identities in Early Iron Age Europe

During the Early Iron Age, significant changes are apparent in the ways people used their material culture to communicate information about differences – between individuals, communities and regions. They also marked status more elaborately than before and linked high status closely with long-distance contacts. We can examine these changes best by viewing them in the context of greater mobility of persons and more intensive circulation of goods within Europe and throughout greater Eurasia and the Mediterranean basin. New concepts of the human person in relation to the social and natural environments are suggested both by patterns of objects arranged in burials and by the increased use of figurines during this period (Figure 1).

## Concept and character of the Iron Age

The 'Iron Age' is an idea created by researchers in the nineteenth century as a means of organizing materials from later prehistoric sites in Europe. It was defined as the period between the time that iron first came into general use and the Roman conquests. For the central regions of temperate Europe, the Iron Age began around 800 BC; in Britain and Scandinavia, around 600 BC, and later in some areas.

Other changes besides the development of iron technology

distinguish the Iron Age from the Bronze Age. In many parts of Europe, larger communities developed, reflected in manufacturing and trading centres and in richly equipped burials in often monumental funerary structures. Increased interaction between peoples in different regions contributed to change, including ways people shaped and expressed their identities. The first Greek written accounts that mention peoples of temperate Europe date from the sixth and fifth centuries BC.

Since the beginnings of systematic archaeological research in the nineteenth century, approaches to the Iron Age have been strongly normative. Investigators have aimed at working out typological and chronological sequences, defining archaeological 'cultures,' synthesizing evidence for trade and settlement systems in different times and places, and establishing styles and practices considered typical of particular groups. Since the 1960s, as the quantity and quality of archaeological data have increased greatly, and as new perspectives have been brought to examination of the evidence, attention has focused on the extraordinary diversity of social organization, human behaviour and cultural expression in Iron Age Europe.

## New patterns of material expression

The interplay between changes that were happening internally within the societies of temperate Europe and changes elsewhere in greater Eurasia created circumstances in which people developed new ideas about who they were and how they related to other individuals and groups. Changes are apparent in the identity of the individual, of the community, of communities within regions and in groups of high-status persons.

Several kinds of evidence indicate a change in the idea and expression of the identity of the individual. In central parts of the continent, tumulus burial replaced flat graves for many persons in the Early Iron Age. Constructing a tumulus over a

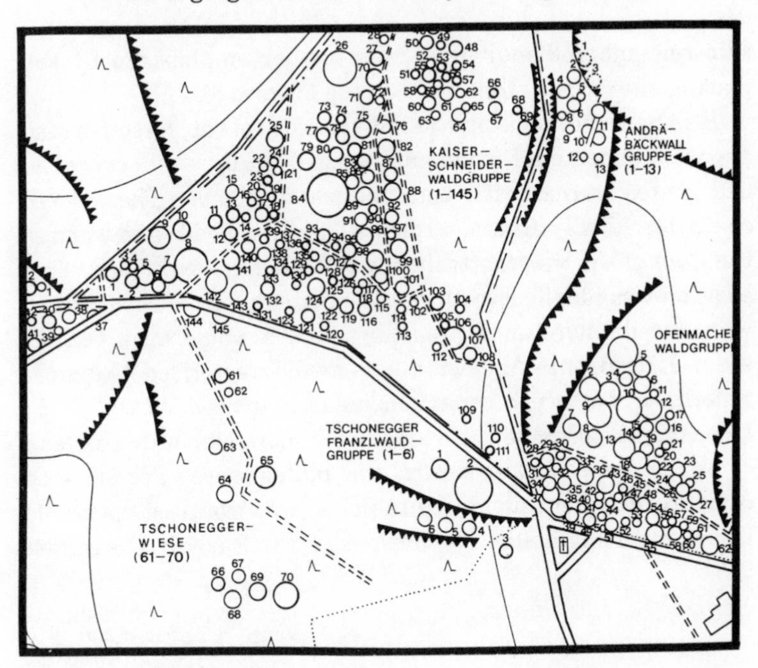


2. Plan of part of the Early Iron Age cemetery at Kleinklein, Austria, showing individual burial mounds. Note the great variability in size.

grave served to draw attention to the individual and to the individual's family and kin group, and to convey messages about their relation to the rest of society. Structure, size and form of tumuli varied, providing a complex medium for communication of information about individuals and the groups to which they belonged (Figure 2). In the earlier part of the Early Iron Age, mounds were most often intended for a single burial. In the later part, larger tumuli often accommodated multiple burials. Usually the central burial was distinguished by many features from the other graves, a practice that can be understood in terms of changes in status identity (see below). In some instances, the linking of the mound as monument with a specific remembered individual was further emphasized by the placing of a carved stone stele on top (Figure 3).

This new emphasis on the individuality of the person is also apparent in personal ornaments, such as the broad sheet bronze belt plates buried with both men and women. These were characteristically around 40 cm long by 15 cm wide and worn at the front of the waist, attached to a leather or textile belt. This location was ideally sited for transmitting information, since it was placed where an approaching person would most readily see it. Late Bronze Age belt plates are characterized by simple repetitious patterned ornament, usually incised. In the Early Iron Age, the ornament became much more elaborate. Instead of simple repeating patterns, the plates were covered with complex ornament divided into fields, with contrasting motifs in neighbouring fields. The designs on the Early Iron Age belt

3. Reconstruction drawing of the Hirschlanden statue, set on top of the burial mound at the base of which it was found.

plates were typically executed in repoussé rather than incising, a more laborious technique representing a greater investment of specialized craft skill. If these objects communicated information about the wearer, then the more complex patterning of the Early Iron Age implies that differentiating the individual from others was more important that it had been previously. Similar changes can be observed in fibulae, another common kind of personal ornament, worn on the chest or shoulder, where it was easily seen by others.

During the Early Iron Age we can recognize greater efforts by communities to express their identities through their material culture. In many regions, the practice of enclosing farmsteads by boundary ditches and sometimes with palisades, thus marking off the settlement from surrounding land, became common at this time. Although neighbouring communities typically shared forms of pottery, types of personal ornaments, clothing styles and burial practices, close examination reveals that each expressed its uniqueness. For example, in a recent study investigators compared an Early Iron Age cemetery at Dattingen in southwest Germany with the nearby cemetery in the huge Magdalenenberg tumulus. In the community that buried its dead at the Magdalenenberg, the common practice was to bury men with two categories of personal ornaments – belts with bronze belt plates, and fibulae – and with weapons. At Dattingen, weapons, belt plates and fibulae were not placed in men's graves. Thus neighbouring communities that shared common material cultures chose distinctly different practices in the communication of information in the funerary ritual.

The formation of regionally recognizable groupings of communities in the course of the Early Iron Age is an important indication of large-scale changes taking place. During the Late Bronze Age, the peoples of the central part of the continent that is the focus of this book created a material culture that archaeologists have called the North Alpine Tradition. During the

Early Iron Age in this same region, investigators recognize several distinct regional groups, including the Hallstatt group in southern central Europe, the Nordic in northern central Europe and the Lausitz in northeastern Europe, each defined by particular kinds of pottery, metal ornaments and burial practice. Within these groups, investigators define sub-groups. The Hallstatt group is subdivided into the West Hallstatt and the East Hallstatt; Lausitz into the Silesian, Görlitz, Billendorf and House-Urn groups. The sub-dividing goes on, as archaeologists recognize regionally distinctive features of pottery forms, jewellery types and burial practice that communities developed in the course of the Early Iron Age.

In contrast to representations on maps drawn by archaeologists, none of these regional groups exhibits sharp boundaries, nor does any show uniform adherence to specific rules of behaviour. For example, the Hallstatt groups in southern central Europe are characterized by burial mounds and a shift from cremation to inhumation, the Lausitz and Nordic groups in the north by cremation and flat graves. But some Lausitz and Nordic graves have small mounds, and recent research reveals that many graves of the Hallstatt regions were flat, situated between mounds. Graves in the Hallstatt area often contain substantial amounts of metal jewellery, including ornate bronze fibulae used to fasten clothing on the shoulder or chest. In the northern groups, metal jewellery is much less common, and more often consists of straight pins instead of fibulae. But some fibulae occur in northern burials, and some straight pins in southern.

This archaeological evidence suggests that on the one hand, peoples in particular regions were developing their own particular ways of doing things – ways that served as signs of their distinctiveness. On the other hand, the fact that there was variability throughout, and no sharp boundaries in burial practice or material culture, indicates that considerable movement of people and circulation of material took place. Within every region, practices varied.

In the Early Iron Age, burial practices were used as an arena for the representation of status differences to a much greater extent than in preceding times. In different parts of Europe, communities used different media for expressing these distinctions. Common to many regions, but with considerable local variability, were large mounds of earth, inhumation burial, wooden chambers, weapons (for males), elaborate personal ornaments, gold, feasting equipment and vehicles. In western central Europe, characteristic media were ornate daggers, gold neck rings and other ring jewellery, Greek and Etruscan feasting vessels and four-wheeled wagons. In east-central Europe, special status was represented by often enormous burial mounds, as at Hartnermichelkogel near Kleinklein in Austria, and in the graves were placed ornate swords and spears, horse-riding equipment and even horses. Rich tombs in the central Balkans, such as Glasinac, Novi Pazar and Trebenište, are characterized by ornate Greek bronze vessels, gold ornaments and amber carvings. Further east, among the Ferigile group of Romania, status was communicated through burials containing a variety of often ornate weapons, including double-axes, hammer-axes, arrows and daggers, as well as horse-riding gear and wagons. North of the Black Sea, under the massive tumuli known as kurgans, rich graves contained great quantities of lavishly ornamented goldwork, much of it decoration on weapons or related to feasting, along with Greek pottery, ornate horse-riding equipment and often horses.

Thus sets of symbols employed to represent status identity varied regionally, but the phenomenon of lavish expression of status differences was common throughout southern regions of the continent, particularly in the latter half of the Early Iron Age.

## Mobility and interaction: growing knowledge of the other

We can begin to understand the character of the changes outlined above if we examine the larger historical context in which they took place. The key process behind the observed changes was rapidly increasing interaction between communities and between regions. The southern imports of fine ceramic and bronze vessels from Greece and Italy have long been a focus of attention in Early Iron Age Europe. Other goods such as amber, coral, graphite, glass and copper and tin, have also been part of the discussion. But that discourse has been too narrowly focused.

There was much more mobility in prehistoric Europe than the dominant paradigm suggests. Long-distance trade was becoming important already in the Neolithic Period, and in the Bronze Age trade in copper and tin, glass, graphite and amber grew in intensity. Several recent studies highlight indications of highly mobile individuals in Bronze Age Europe.

In the Early Iron Age, there is abundant evidence of a wide variety of objects found far from their places of origin, transmitted through different mechanisms such as trade, family exchanges and raiding. In addition to the much-discussed Greek and Etruscan luxury objects, bronze ornaments, ceramics and other objects circulated. A cemetery recently excavated at Ilse near Petershagen in northwestern Germany provides an example. In a region in which the dominant burial practice was cremation with very few grave goods, archaeologists excavated fifteen inhumation graves, thirteen of them outfitted with considerable metal jewellery. Most individuals wore large wire earrings and rings on both ankles. Other goods included hairpins, bracelets, fibulae, glass and amber beads and toilet articles. These objects are characteristic of the mid-sixth century BC in the upper Rhine region, 500 km to the south, where inhumation was the dominant burial practice at this time. The character of the grave goods in the thirteen graves with goods suggests that those individuals were women (based on associations when skeletal preservation is good); for the two without goods, there is so far no indication of sex. These graves may represent a community that moved from the upper Rhine northward to the edge of the North European Plain. Or they may represent a local community that adopted jewellery traditions and burial practice from a group with which they were in contact to the south. In either case, this cemetery is a demonstration of the greater mobility of individuals during the Early Iron Age.

Mobility among elite groups is well illustrated by the 'Scythian'-style materials found at Witaszkowo (Vettersfelde) in Poland. The precise nature of the find is unclear, but the character of the objects strongly suggests a man's burial in the tradition of the Iron Age horse-riding peoples of the Eurasian steppes 1500 km or more to the east. The gold fish in elaborate animal-style ornament was accompanied by a short sword in an ornate gold-covered scabbard, a long iron sword with gold scabbard mount and a variety of gold ornaments that include a plaque, pendant, earring, bracelet and chain. The style of all of the objects links them with 'Scythian' tombs of around 500 BC, but it is not clear whether these were manufactured in the steppe region or somewhere further west. In any case, the find is a striking demonstration of mobility between the steppes and east-central Europe around 500 BC.

The movement of objects throughout Europe needs to be understood within a larger geographical context. Peoples of greater Eurasia, including the Levant, the Aegean, Italy, Gaul, Iberia and the lands north of the Alps can be seen to experience an intensifying of contact and interaction. An increase in the scale of commerce is evident throughout much of the Mediterranean basin. Sherratt and Sherratt argue that entrepreneurial merchant enterprise began to supplant palace economies as a motivating force behind the growth in trade, leading to accumulation of wealth on a much larger scale than before. The 'imports', finds of which link the Levant with northern Europe, Greece with Britain and Italy with the Rhineland, are signs that larger numbers of people were travelling, trading and sharing information between regions.

## Archaeological sites as moments in process

Iron Age studies have developed in a paradigm that focuses on the analysis of excavated sites and of objects recovered from them. Research projects and resultant publications examine specific cemeteries and settlements and make comparisons between them. The image that emerges is of static, fixed communities that inhabited the settlements and buried their dead in the cemeteries over generations. Foreign goods are typically conceived in terms of imports brought in by merchants and exchanged for local products. This emphasis on research at single sites, often with little attention to other settlements and cemeteries in the immediate area, has led to a static conception of the cultural landscape of Iron Age Europe.

Social boundaries of communities surely were much more fluid than most models suggest. Individuals left home to marry, to go on trading expeditions, to participate in raiding parties and to start new communities. Visitors, including travelling merchants and perhaps pilgrims staying a night and relatives lingering longer, contributed to the dynamism of many communities. The appearance of objects of outside origin on settlements and in graves reflects such mobility.

## Interaction and identity

Identity becomes an important factor when individuals and groups come into contact with others who are different. Interaction creates knowledge of the other, and around that knowledge persons and groups fashion identities and means of expressing them. The increasing interaction during the Early Iron Age evident in the context of greater mobility created circumstances in which individuals and groups became more aware of their special characteristics as they encountered increasing numbers of others. Individually distinctive belt plates, fibulae, swords and daggers can be understood in terms of identity expression on the inter-community level. For the patterns to communicate information about the individual, all concerned needed to know the code.

The development of regional populations that shared particular practices can be understood in terms of the greater interaction on the regional level. For example, increasing interaction between peoples east of the middle Elbe River led groups in neighbouring regions to create distinctive material expressions of their identities. In one region, communities created house-shaped ceramic vessels based on a model from Italy that they used as burial urns. These objects were part of a funerary ritual that included construction of chamber graves of stone slabs. Neighbouring communities to the east, known as the Billendorf group, did not share those distinctive funerary vessels or burial chambers, but instead created their own distinguishing ceramic vessels. One form was a large open-mouthed pot with high conical neck, ornamented with horizontal and oblique incised lines and small knobs on the shoulder, used both for food preparation and in funerary ceremony. The other was a short jug with broad, high handle. Inter-community distinctiveness was probably expressed through many aspects of the funerary ritual, but in the present state of research we have only the pottery and grave structures as recognizable signs of these differences.

## Imports, elites and regionality

The representation of elite status in richly outfitted burials all across southern temperate Europe, from Iberia to the Urals, can also be understood in terms of changes in identity during this time of intensifying interaction. As Mary Helms has shown, long-distance interaction is closely linked to status and identity, and circulating goods provide means for individuals and groups to gain status and power. In the dynamic and fluid social context of Early Iron Age Europe, we need to understand rich burials not as reflections of a static hierarchical society, but as representations of moments within a process of social expression and display among the living. These graves are complex structures, and they express identity on different levels.

The undisturbed and exceptionally well excavated burial at Hochdorf near Stuttgart provides a good example. The 30-year-old man was buried around 530 BC. This individual is identified as elite, accorded greater wealth and status than most people in his society. The large mound, elaborate oak burial chamber, abundant gold, special dagger, numerous pieces of feasting equipment, ornate textiles and bronze couch all indicate special status and wealth (Figure 4). These material manifestations set him off from the rest of his community. Some of these special objects connect this man with other elite individuals in this landscape northwest of the Alps. The gold neck ring is a standard emblem, and similar but not identical rings have been recovered in about 40 graves. The ornate dagger, four-wheeled wagon and feasting equipment also are parts of a standard set of status signs that mark these graves. Yet within this special group, the objects at Hochdorf identify this individual as unusual.

The nine ornate drinking horns on the south wall of the chamber, one exceptionally large made of iron with gold bands, the others of natural aurochs horn, are unique to Hochdorf.

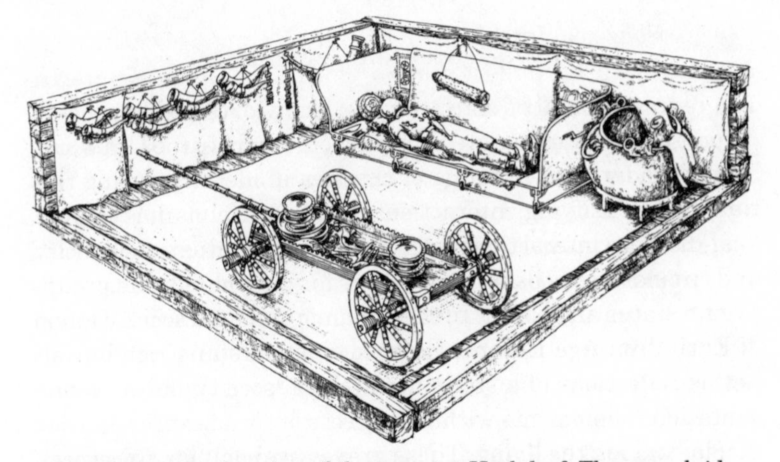

4. Reconstruction drawing of the grave at Hochdorf. The man, laid out on a bronze couch, wears numerous signs of his special status – neck ring, fibulae, belt plate and shoe ornaments, all of gold, and the scabbard holding his dagger is coated with gold. At his feet is a large bronze cauldron from a Greek workshop, and on top of it a gold bowl. On the south wall hang nine drinking horns – at his head, an exceptionally large iron horn decorated with gold bands, the other eight consist of aurochs horns with ornamental metal fittings. In the foreground is a wagon, laden with objects that include nine bronze dishes.

They match in number nine bronze dishes arranged on the wagon. Krausse interprets these nine sets as representing the buried leader and eight followers. Later texts inform us that chiefs in early Europe were expected to host feasts that affirmed the coherence of the group and the status and role of the leader. The cauldron, with a capacity of some 400 litres and residue suggestive of mead, probably represents the beverage that the leader ladled with the gold bowl to fill the horns of his followers. If this interpretation is correct, then this grave composition represents the actions through which the buried individual reaffirmed his identity. Perhaps some of these vessels were used a final time in a funeral feast at the tumulus.

The bronze cauldron and the red dye in some of the textiles in the grave are manifestations of this man's link to Mediterranean societies. Motifs on the textiles are also of Mediterranean origin, but the textiles, some woven together with badger hair, were local products. The large number of bronze figural representations in the grave – three lions on the cauldron, eight female figurines holding the couch, eight warriors represented in repoussé on the back of the couch and figures of horses on the yoke – is unusual for this time and suggests significant adoption of this new element from Mediterranean tradition (see below). All these links with Mediterranean themes are firmly embedded in local funerary practice.

Hochdorf, like all burials, is the materialization of a moment in the process of a funerary ceremony. Quantities of pottery recovered near many rich graves suggest funeral feasting as part of the ritual. A stunning example is at Tovsta Mohyla in southern Ukraine, where large quantities of Greek amphorae and animal bones were found in the ditches associated with the tumulus. At Hochdorf and at kurgans in eastern Europe, special pits in the mounds contain objects that were used during the ceremonies. In 1992, excavations in the cemetery at Vix in eastern France revealed a rectangular enclosure with life-size stone sculptures of a richly adorned woman and a well-outfitted male warrior, situated next to an entrance into the enclosure (Figure 5). The neck ring on the statue of the woman is similar to that in the rich woman's grave; perhaps this statue was a representation of that person. Large quantities of pottery and skulls of animals found in association with the enclosure may be remains of funerary ceremonies there. This newly emerging evidence for part of the mortuary ritual in and near tumuli helps in the understanding of the burials as material remains of dynamic processes, not static representations of social structure.

Greek and Etruscan imports have featured largely in discus-

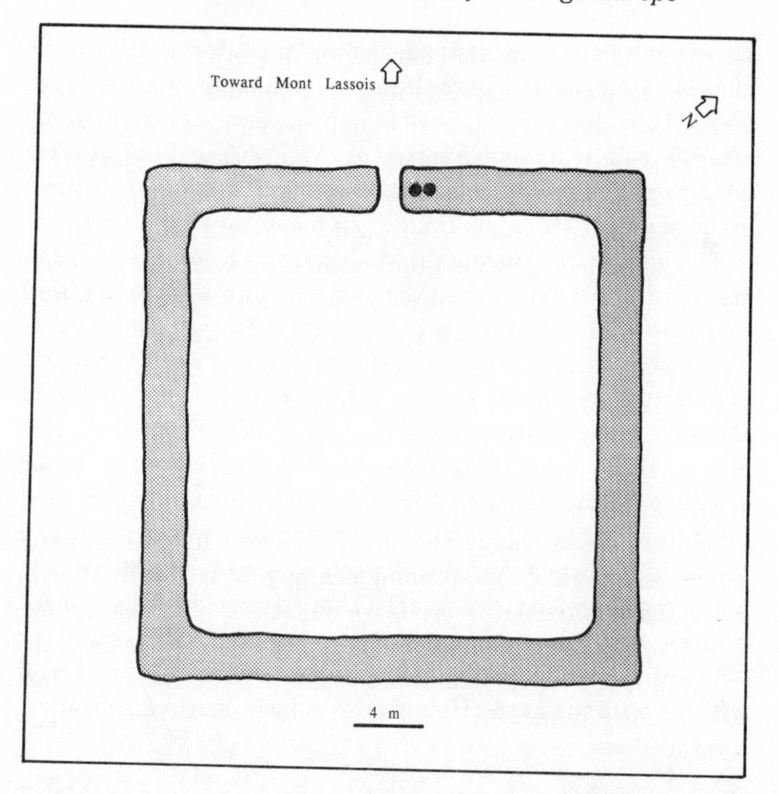


5. Schematic sketch plan of the enclosure in the cemetery at Vix, situated 200 m southwest of the rich woman's burial. The square enclosure, about 23 m each side, is defined by a ditch, shown here by shading. At the middle of the northwest side, facing Mont Lassois, is a break in the ditch 1.2 m wide, apparently an entrance into the interior. The black circles mark the locations of the two carved stone figures; the sculpture of the woman was closest to the entrance.

sions of the Early Iron Age, but in light of the foregoing discussion their significance needs to be re-evaluated. Most significant is not their purpose in their societies of origin, but the roles they played in the Iron Age societies, as materializations of social relations. As foreign objects, they embodied knowledge of distant places, peoples and practices, which lent an aura of cosmopolitanism to those who possessed and displayed them. They signalled affiliation among geographically separated elite individuals. These Greek and Etruscan imports were among a wide range of objects that were circulating at this time, many of which served to link people across large distances.

The appearance during the sixth century BC of larger settlements displaying unusually active manufacturing and commercial activity, such as El Berrueco in Iberia, Mont Lassois in eastern France, the Heuneburg in southwest Germany, Stična in Slovenia and Belsk in the middle Dnieper region in Ukraine, can be understood in the context of the increasing role of foreign objects in the assertion and display of status. These centres were mechanisms through which competing elites could direct the circulation systems that provided the desired foreign goods. Rich burials preceded the emergence of the centres, and many regions with rich burials do not seem to have settlement centres. Some centres served also as arenas for display, along with the funerary rituals, as in the case of the clay-brick wall with its bastions at the Heuneburg and the enormous fortifications at Belsk.

### Iconography and identity: new representations

During the Early Iron Age, representations of humans, which are rare from Bronze Age contexts, became increasingly common, especially from the beginning of the sixth century BC onwards. Small bronze figurines include those in the scene on the Strettweg wagon (Figure 6), as horseback riders at Hallstatt and the eight figures supporting the couch at Hochdorf. Incised pictures of humans on pottery are common in central and east-central Europe, for example at Sopron in Hungary. Life-size stone sculptures are associated with sites linked with rich burials, as at Hirschlanden and Vix. This new practice of repre-

6. Reconstruction drawing of the bronze wagon from a rich man's grave at Strettweg in Steiermark, Austria, dated at about 600 BC. The representations of the woman in the centre and of the men on foot and on horseback around her are characteristic of human figurines of the Early Iron Age. The woman wears an ornamental belt and earrings. The men wear no personal ornaments, but many hold weapons – spears, battle-axes, helmets and shields. The figure of the woman in the centre is 22.6 cm high.

senting the human form is a significant innovation, and it suggests important changes in the ways that people thought about themselves in relation to the world they lived in.

The immediate inspiration for these representations may have been the arts of Greece during the seventh and sixth centuries BC. The abundant small bronze figurines from the Greek world may have served as models for the bronze figurines in temperate Europe, painted figures on Greek pottery for the incised figures on Early Iron Age pottery and the Greek *kouri* and Etruscan statues as models for the Hirschlanden and related sculptures. These human portrayals must have had a significant impact on the peoples of temperate Europe. The bronze figurines and stone sculptures are closely associated with elite contexts in which display was an important aspect. It is likely that these representations were viewed by, and formed an impression on, all of the members of the populace who viewed the funerary rituals. A result of this practice was to make the Early Iron Age peoples feel increasingly closely linked with the larger, more complex societies of the Mediterranean world. The use of human figurines enables us to see how they chose to portray themselves – in what associations and with what material accoutrements. Many figurines of women show the same ornaments that identify women in burials. The Strettweg woman and the figures supporting the Hochdorf couch, for example, wear earrings and ornate belts, as do women in well-outfitted graves of the period. Figurines of men, such as those on the Strettweg wagon, the Hirschlanden stele and the sculpture at the Vix enclosure, lack these ornaments and are distinguished by their weapons, as are men in richer burials. The figurines thus provide further evidence for the gender-identification of women and men, at least among those in the wealthy graves, on the basis of different material objects associated with them.

In the Bronze Age, the only animal that was frequently represented was the water bird. In the Early Iron Age, this creature was joined by bulls, stags and horses. Bulls had long been potent symbols in Mediterranean societies, horses were commonly portrayed both in Greece and in the steppe regions north of the Black Sea, and stags were frequently represented in burials in the steppe areas. Like the idea of representing the human form, that of representing these animals probably was stimulated by interaction with groups in the Mediterranean and eastern steppe regions. But for the animal figures as for the human figurines, using models adopted from outside resulted not in efforts to copy foreign forms; rather Iron Age craftworkers created locally meaningful versions. The identity of Iron Age Europeans was becoming ever more interconnected with their ideas about their relationships to the peoples to the south and to the east, defining themselves partly through borrowing themes but also transforming those themes into new ones.

# 3

# Creating Interregional Identities

The start of the Late Iron Age, or La Tène period, is commonly defined by the appearance of a new style of ornament during the fifth century BC. But other important changes are apparent in the ways people conceived and expressed their identities. These new attitudes are particularly expressed in the most richly outfitted burials. After a couple of generations, the new style spread widely throughout Europe. The practice of ritual on a much larger scale, beginning in the fourth century BC, signals a new importance to community and regional identity among peoples in temperate Europe.

## New style of ornament

In central and western parts of Europe, the start of the Late Iron Age is distinguished by the appearance of the La Tène style of ornament. Recent research suggests that the new style developed in the middle Rhineland early in the fifth century BC. While the style of Early Iron Age decoration on metalwork and pottery is characteristically geometric, built upon squares, rhomboids, circles and triangles, La Tène style is floral, asymmetrical and figural. In *Early Celtic Art* (1944), Paul Jacobsthal demonstrated that the motifs that characterize the new style were adapted from decorative patterns on objects from Greek and Etruscan workshops. They include leaves, petals, blossoms,

7. Gold openwork that covered a wooden bowl, from a burial at Schwarzenbach in the Saarland, Germany. Diameter 12.6 cm. This object illustrates the stylized plant forms that characterize early La Tène ornament.

tendrils and faces of animals, humans and monsters (Figure 7). Recent analyses emphasize in addition the importance of ornamental traditions from the steppes of eastern Europe for the creation of La Tène ornament. At about the same time that this style appeared in western central Europe, motifs derived from similar plant elements in Greek ornament entered into the repertoire of decoration in the steppe region north of the Black Sea.

Ludwig Pauli argued that the La Tène style was created by an emerging elite group as a means of displaying status. The earliest expressions of this style are in exceptionally rich burials in the middle Rhineland, and only after a generation or two did a substantial portion of Iron Age societies adopt it. A special early characteristic is the use of stylized representations of humans and animals in gold and bronze ornaments (Figure 8). These representations are different from those of the Early Iron Age. Rather than simple, unadorned portrayals of men and women and of animals such as stags and bulls, now many figures were transformed into the medium of the new style. Male and female representations are often replaced by generic human-like faces (though often moustachioed faces indicate men), and rather than natural animals, many monsters unlike any creatures in nature are shown.

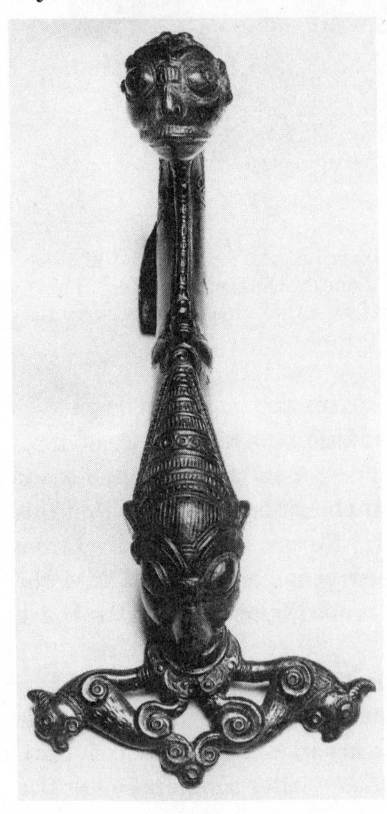

8. Bronze figural fibula from a man's grave at Parsberg in Bavaria, Germany. Length 8.8 cm. Note the stylized representation of the human head at the top and of the three faces of monstrous animals at the bottom.

## Rich burials and the new style

Most of the earliest examples of the new style occur on exceptionally fine products of local metalworking, including gold and bronze ornaments and iron and bronze weapons, and they occur in richly outfitted burials. The greatest concentration of burials that include objects ornamented in the early La Tène style, numbering about 50, are in the middle Rhineland. Another, smaller concentration is in eastern central France between the Aisne and upper Seine rivers, where some 30 are known. Smaller numbers are in Bohemia, Upper Austria and central France. In some respects, the graves, dating between 475 and 400 BC, are similar to the rich burials of the Early Iron Age treated in the preceding chapter. With those earlier graves they share the inhumation practice (in the majority of cases, though a few are cremations), wooden burial chambers, sizeable mounds, wheeled vehicles (two-wheeled chariots or carts now rather than four-wheeled wagons), gold rings and other jewellery, feasting vessels and, in the case of men, weapons. Among these richly outfitted early La Tène burials, there is variation in grave structure, rite (inhumation and cremation) and grave good combinations. Some of this variation is regional – rich graves in the middle Rhineland are characterized by Etruscan bronze vessels, gold ring jewellery and ornate swords (in the men's graves). In central France, gold decorations are less common, but bronze harness ornaments are characteristic, and some ornate helmets occur.

Most of the early La Tène rich graves are situated north of the centres at which the Early Iron Age rich burials occur, but there is some overlap, and in central and eastern France rich graves of the two traditions are in the same regions. Unlike the earlier series, these later ones are not associated with large settlements that yield abundant evidence for manufacturing and trade.

The similar patterns in grave goods in early La Tène rich graves throughout western and central Europe can be understood in terms of the increasing mobility discussed in Chapter 2. Rudolf Echt interprets the men's graves as those of warrior-princes who engaged in regular travel, including raiding campaigns, and maintained strong contacts with others of similar status from central France to Bohemia. Even with some regional variation in burial goods, the basic military equipment in men's graves is quite consistent throughout – sword, lance and helmet. This regularity in the expression of identity closely linked to military themes suggests that the 'martial ideology' of later Iron Age groups might have its origin, or a significant phase in its development, in this context.

Echt's analysis of the corresponding richly equipped women's graves – fewer in number than the men's – suggests that their identity was rooted more in local rather than interregional contexts. In his study of the Reinheim burial, he argues that many of the objects placed with the dead woman relate to a special religious or ritual role, a theme that extends to other well-outfitted women's burials. In the Reinheim grave, the sizeable number of representations of humans and animals, mostly in bronze but also in gold, is noteworthy. This grave also contained one of the earliest bronze mirrors in temperate Europe, an object that became a standard mark of wealthy women's graves later in the Iron Age and one that has implications for the individual's sense of self.

The recently excavated grave at Gündlingen on the upper Rhine in southwest Germany is of special importance in this regard. A well preserved skeleton of an adult woman was accompanied by an above-average set of personal ornaments – four fibulae, two bracelets and two leg rings, all of bronze (Figure 9). One of the bracelets was ornamented with stylized faces and other decoration. Next to her lower left leg was a large number of objects that can be characterized as amulets, prob-

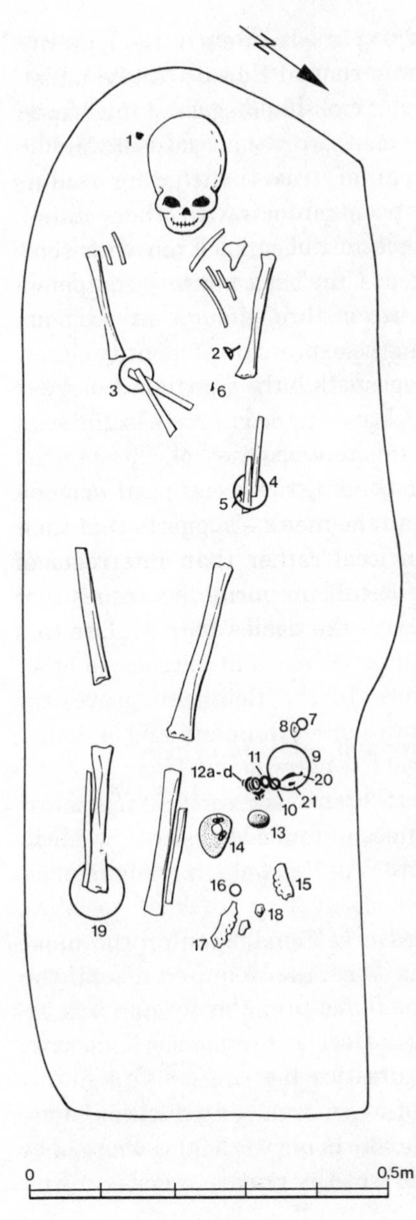


9. Plan of the central burial in mound 3 at Gündlingen in Baden-Württemberg, Germany. The skeleton of an adult woman was accompanied by characteristic jewellery. Unusual is the deposit of objects linked to healing or magic, situated next to her lower left leg. 1, 2, 5, 6 bronze fibulae. 3, 4 bronze bracelets. 7, 9, 10, 16 bronze rings. 8 geode. 11 amber bead. 12a bronze figurine of a bull. 12b bronze ring with cross. 12c amber ring. 13 egg-shaped pebble. 14 flat piece of limestone with natural perforation, repaired with bronze bands. 15, 17 dog's upper and lower jaws. 18 ceramic sherd. 19 iron leg ring. 20 miniature bronze knife. 21 dog tooth.

ably originally deposited in a bag or box. They include a naturally perforated stone that had been mended with bronze strips, two bronze rings, a geode, an egg-shaped pebble, a bronze figurine of a bull, amber beads and two dog jaws. In the Middle Ages and into modern times, all of these objects were used as amulets or charms to protect people from harm, to cure illness and to bring good luck. The placement of such objects in this well-outfitted woman's grave at Gündlingen may have identified her as a specialist in the healing arts or in religious practices.

In eastern Europe, archaeologists have recognized a great increase in the numbers of richly equipped burials in the kurgans of the fifth century BC. The categories of objects that distinguish these graves from the majority are similar to those of the preceding century in the region (see Chapter 2), but some burials were now much richer than before, and new styles of ornament are represented. Some of the mounds were sites of much more elaborate mortuary ceremonies than earlier (see below).

## New attitudes toward self and other

The structure of burial assemblages in the early La Tène context indicates important changes in attitude toward the Mediterranean societies, and changes in the ways that indigenous elites created their identities in relation to those societies. Many of the rich burials of the Early Iron Age contained unique bronze vessels from the Greek world that required exceptional effort, skill and material to manufacture. The outstanding example is the Vix krater, but the Hochdorf cauldron, the bronze tripod and ivory and amber furniture pieces from Grafenbühl and the hydria from Grächwil in Switzerland are other examples of complex and unique products of Greek workshops. The Mediterranean imports in the wealthy graves associated with the early La Tène style, on the other hand, were mainly objects that were part of everyday life of the well-to-do in Greek and Etruscan societies.

While Early Iron Age elites emphasized their status through lavish Mediterranean imports in their graves, their successors emphasized theirs through unique local products, particularly gold neck and arm jewellery. The gold neck rings from Reinheim, Besseringen, Erstfeld and Glauberg (see below) embody elaborate workmanship and are all distinctly different in ornamental form. Though not of solid metal, these early La Tène gold neck rings are considerably thicker and heavier than the majority of the Early Iron Age neck rings, which are similar to one another and are made of thin sheet metal rolled to form a ring. The ring in the rich woman's burial at Vix is exceptional and in many ways more like the early La Tène neck rings than the others of the Early Iron Age.

These changes in imports and in neck rings indicate an important shift in the ways that elites expressed their identities and at the same time a change in attitudes about European Iron Age societies in relation to the Mediterranean peoples. In the early La Tène period, that link became less important to status display, and distinctive local products assumed a greater role in communicating these ideas. In early La Tène burials, we find some imported ceramic and bronze vessels that were transformed by local craftworkers by the addition of elements in La Tène style, and new forms of vessels that are local versions of imported objects. For example, the character of the two Attic *kylikes* from the burial at Kleinaspergle near Stuttgart was transformed through the application of sheet gold ornaments, attached with small bronze pins, to both the exterior and interior surfaces, resulting in an appearance different from that of the original cups (Figure 10). These additions were apparently made in the course of repair work on the vessels. By applying gold La Tène ornaments to ceramic wine cups made in Greece,

10. Greek red-figure *kylix* from burial at Kleinaspergle near Stuttgart, Germany; view of bottom of the vessel. Important is the application of gold ornaments in La Tène style (compare Figure 7, p. 55) to this bowl made in Greece. Diameter of bowl (without handles) 15.5 cm.

the local craftworkers transformed the objects from emblems of interaction between the local elites and the Greek world to signs of those elites' new sense of identity that relied less on display of Mediterranean imports and more on display of their own ornamental system. Other examples are La Tène ornament incised into the surface of Etruscan bronze vessels from Armsheim, Laumersheim and Weiskirchen, and on one without known provenance in the museum at Besançon. Locally-made adaptations of imported vessels include versions of Greek *kylikes* from Plzeň-Roudná and of Etruscan jugs in bronze from Kleinaspergle, Basse-Yutz and Glauberg and in pottery from the Dürrnberg. This process of transforming imported objects is significant in signalling a new attitude towards the role of

Mediterranean imagery in the expression of status identity among elites in temperate Europe. From the start of the fourth century BC, objects imported from Greece and Etruria were much less common north of the Mediterranean. The decrease in imports is apparent across the whole of temperate Europe, from Iberia through western and central Europe to the eastern regions of Ukraine to the Urals. No doubt we could find multiple causes of this decline, both in temperate Europe and in Greece and Etruria. The point I wish to argue here is that the decline resulted at least in part from the decrease in the importance of imports in the structuring of identity among elites in temperate Europe. The replacement of imports altogether in elite funerary display is apparent in the burial complex at the Glauberg in Hesse, Germany.

Recent excavations at the Glauberg provide valuable insight into changes in the expression of identity among rich early La Tène burials. In the case of a great many of the rich graves, the discoveries were made in the nineteenth century, and little information is available about the positions of objects or about above-ground monuments. At the Glauberg, investigations included not only excavation of the mound with two significant graves in it, but also aerial reconaissance, geophysical prospection and extensive, ongoing investigation of the landscape around the tumulus.

Just below a hilltop fortified with an enclosing wall, aerial reconnaissance in 1988 revealed discolouration in agricultural fields that indicated a circular ditch such as frequently occurs around burial mounds. The mound was 48 m in diameter, perhaps about 6 m high originally, and the ditch proved to be about 10 m wide and up to 3.7 m deep. Excavation of the mound in 1994 and 1995 uncovered two graves, both of early La Tène date. Grave 1, inside a wooden chamber beneath a stone covering, contained the skeletal remains of a man about 30 years of age, buried on his back in an extended position with his head to the south. He was buried with weapons, gold ornaments and a bronze drinking vessel. The weapons included an iron sword in a bronze scabbard, two iron lances and a shield. Gold ornaments included an elaborate gold neck ring, a gold bracelet on his right wrist, a gold ring on the ring finger of his right hand and two small gold rings near the head. An ornate bronze jug of local manufacture was in the grave. A bronze animal fibula, two other bronze fibulae and a bronze belt hook were also present. Grave 2, inside a wooden box, contained cremated remains with an iron sword in an iron scabbard with bronze trim, an ornate bronze vessel with tube spout, a bronze fibula and a bronze belt hook.

With the presence of swords and ornate bronze vessels in both graves, and especially the complete set of weaponry and all of the gold in Grave 1, these burials belong to the category of exceptionally rich early La Tène graves. Grave 1 is a striking example of the 'elite warrior' theme. The variability among graves in this category is illustrated here by the absence of signs of wheeled vehicles and of imported vessels from the Mediterranean world. The rich display of figural ornament is of special note. Both of the bronze vessels are elaborately decorated with animal and human figures of cast bronze, and the animal fibula in Grave 1 is a prime example of that group of ornaments.

The objects in these graves that express status identity were removed from the community's gaze at the time of burial but remained in memory. But the Glauberg complex also includes two different kinds of monumental expression that remained visible on the surface of the cultural landscape. Just northwest of the mound the excavations revealed ditches and postholes that indicate that the mound was part of a complex structured landscape (Figure 11). At the bottom of a ditch just west of the mound, next to three large postholes, was a lifesize (1.86 m high) statue of a man sculpted from local sandstone (see cover photograph), broken off at the ankles like the Hirschlanden figure (see Figure 3, p. 38). Features of this statue match objects in Grave 1, just as ornaments on the stone sculpture at Vix seem to match those in the rich woman's grave there (Chapter 2). The neck ring on the Glauberg statue is similar to that in the grave. In addition to bearing body armour, the figure wears a sword on his right side and holds a shield in front of him. He wears a bracelet on his right wrist and a ring on the ring finger of his right hand, matching the jewellery found in Grave 1. On his upper left arm are three bracelets. The details portrayed on this statue suggest that the mound and the complex of which it was part were marked with this monumental sculpture of the man in Grave 1.

Near this statue were found 127 fragments of three additional statues, all apparently similar in size and execution. The association of these four life-size stone statues with the configurations of large postholes suggests that some kind of ceremonial precinct was created next to the mound in connection with the burials. As analysis of the Glauberg site progresses, it will be important to compare this evidence with that from the enclosure at Vix discussed in Chapter 2 (Figure 5, p. 49). It is important that we are now finding that the rich burials were only a part of complex cultural landscapes that played roles in the ceremonies in which status identity was created, reaffirmed and expressed. The Glauberg find also raises questions about the interpretation of the Hirschlanden statue (Figure 2, p. 37). The nearly complete Glauberg statue and that from Hirschlanden are about the same size, both were broken at the ankles and both were recovered at the base of their respective mounds. Did they originally stand on top of the mounds, as the reconstruction in Figure 2 suggests; did they stand in special places just beyond the mounds; or were the similar figures arranged in different ways at the two cemetery complexes?

The Glauberg statue, as well as in the fragments of the others, does not have the character of a portrait of a specific

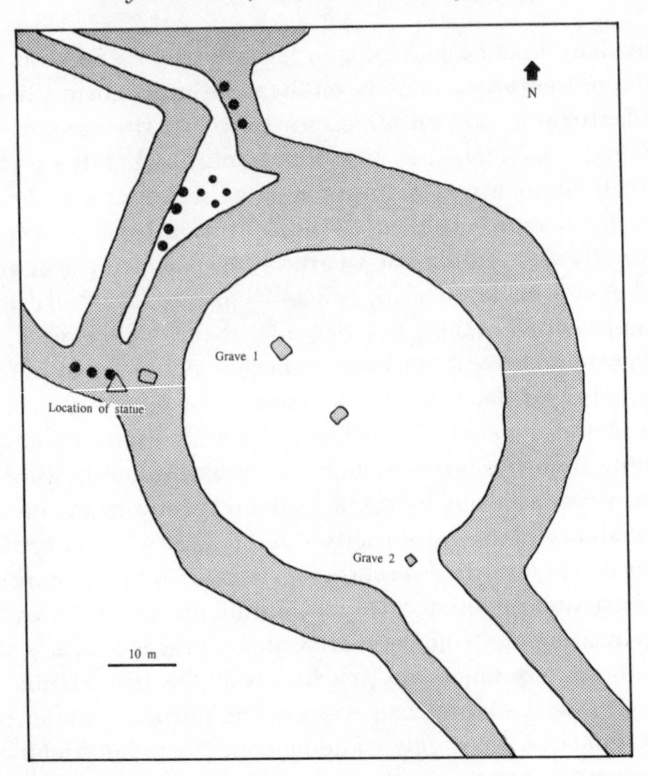


11. Schematic drawing showing the Glauberg tumulus and its immediate surroundings. Shaded areas represent ditches and pits. At the centre of the tumulus, the excavators found an empty pit. Graves 1 and 2 were situated at opposite edges of the tumulus. The ditch that surrounded the tumulus connected with ditches that formed a complex pattern northwest of the mound and the long avenue extending to the southeast. Patterns of postholes within the ditches, and on the surface between them, suggest that structures stood on these locations. The life-size sandstone statue of an armed man, shown in the photograph on the cover of this book, was found in the ditch complex, next to the row of three large posts just west of the mound; the location is marked by a triangle. Fragments of three other similar statues were near this almost complete figure. The rectangle to the right of the triangle represents an empty pit discovered at the bottom of the ditch. The postholes are shown larger here than they actually were.

individual. Like human faces in La Tène metalwork, this stylized representation suggests the idea of a human being, but not the features of a specific person. However, the similarity in personal ornaments and weapons between the statue and the individual in Grave 1 suggests that the statue may have been intended to represent that individual.

Finally, the tumulus was part of an elaborately structured landscape on a large scale. About 40 m westsouthwest of the mound was a rectangular enclosure about 9 by 9 m in size, defined by a ditch. Its purpose is unclear. Some 250 m south of the mound was another, smaller mound that contained a burial that included weapons, a gold ring and an ornate fibula. Extending from the larger tumulus in a southeasterly direction was an avenue about 10 m wide defined by parallel ditches 7 m wide (shown in the lower right corner of Figure 11) that run for about 350 m, at which point the western ditch turns sharply to the west, and eastern to the east. The ditches are still about 2.8 deep in the subsoil, indicating that this landscape feature must have been very imposing. It is not clear how this avenue was used, whether just for the event of the burial of one or both individuals, or repeatedly for ceremonial purposes. Significant is the outlay of human energy required to create this monumental funerary landscape and the permanence and high visibility accorded these signs of the buried individuals' status. The fact that locally produced elite goods replaced imported objects as signs for elite display could help to explain the lack of commercial centres such as Mont Lassois and the Heuneburg in association with these later rich burials. If the centres served mainly to generate goods – both collected and manufactured – for export to the Mediterranean world to insure a supply of politically-important imports (see above), then a decline in the social significance of those imports could have made such centres superfluous.

## Spread of the La Tène style

The practice of outfitting burials with lavish goods, wooden chambers and substantial mounds declined after 400 BC, and the flat inhumation cemeteries of the following centuries indicate a much less differentiated distribution of wealth in graves. During the fourth and third centuries BC, the La Tène style spread widely throughout Europe, from the middle Rhineland and eastern France to Portugal in the west, Ukraine in the east, Italy in the south and Britain and Sweden in the north. This dissemination of the new style from its social origins in a small group of richly outfitted graves in west-central Europe, to a broad spectrum of the population over most of temperate Europe, is a striking phenomenon with significant implications for issues of identity. While we no longer accept the idea that this stylistic dissemination represents the 'spread of the Celts', the widespread adoption of this style surely indicates the formation of a shared identity on some level. The style became common throughout the central regions of temperate Europe, and its use on personal ornaments, weapons and pottery distinguished their possessors from peoples on the shores of the Mediterranean to their south and on the North European Plain to their north. This increasing uniformity across much of temperate Europe is apparent in other practices as well.

In his study of early La Tène (roughly 475-300/250 BC) cemeteries from central France to Transylvania (not including the rich burials from the beginning of this phase discussed above), Lorenz shows that burial practice was strikingly uniform. Inhumation was dominant, with the deceased usually extended on the back. Grave goods included ring jewellery, especially ornamenting the neck, upper and lower arm and leg, fibulae and weapons, mainly lance points and swords, and pottery. Within this broad uniformity, Lorenz identifies regional groupings based on grave orientation and specific combinations of grave goods, as well as minor variations in the La Tène style. This general uniformity of burial practice and style represents a change from the regionally distinctive patterns of the Early Iron Age (Chapter 2).

In the middle La Tène phase (300/250-150 BC), Lorenz notes an increase in numbers of swords in burials, and fibulae are much more generally distributed in cemeteries. Bronze link belts, often ornamented with enamel inlay and with horse-head hooks, are a common feature of women's graves. Burial practices were strikingly similar in hundreds of excavated cemeteries across the central regions of temperate Europe, with similar grave pits, coffins or burial boards and combinations of fibulae, neck, arm and finger rings, belt hooks, link belts, weapons and pottery. The La Tène style on objects in these cemeteries is similar, but not identical, across the continent. Regional variations make apparent that we are not seeing the results of widespread migration, but rather sharing, borrowing and adopting. For example, in two well-equipped burials in a cemetery at Iwanowice in southern Poland, Woźniak notes that the composition of the sets of weapons are the same as those throughout the whole La Tène region, but that the ornamentation on objects in the graves shows local manufacture, not importation or introduction through migration. The same applies to finds with La Tène style materials further east, in Bulgaria, Romania, Moldova and Ukraine.

In investigations of questions of wealth and status in cemeteries of this period, there are no clear criteria by which to divide groups into richer or poorer, higher and lower status. Instead there is a wide range of variability in the outfitting of burials. Weapons are common in men's graves, suggesting that military activity was a prominent aspect of cultural life now for a larger proportion of men than before.

Many of the most lavish examples of La Tène style are found at the outer edges of its distribution. If the style was being used as an identifier to distinguish peoples of temperate Europe from their northern and southern neighbours, then these examples from the peripheries of the La Tène zone may represent a phenomenon frequently observed in situations in which members of a group live in an environment in which they feel their identity threatened by more numerous others. In fourth and third centuries BC Europe, this phenomenon is illustrated by four ornate helmets recovered on the western, southern and eastern edges of the distribution of La Tène ornament. Two western examples, from a cave deposit at Agris in southwest France and from the Seine River at Amfreville, come from contexts suggestive of ritual deposition and are dated to the second half of the fourth century BC. The Canosa helmet from southern Italy (Figure 12) was part of a weapon assemblage in a burial dated to the same time. The iron helmet from Ciumeşti in Romania, ornamented with an extraordinary bronze bird of prey with movable wings, was also part of a weapon grave assemblage and is dated to the third century BC.

## Public ritual

Beginning in the fourth century BC, groups throughout Europe began depositing objects on a scale much greater than before in contexts that archaeologists link with ritual. Evidence for ritual deposition is abundant in the Late Bronze Age, but in the great majority of cases, deposits were modest in scale and were made either in natural locations, such as ponds, lakes, bogs, rivers, caves and beneath cliffs, or in disused wells. In the Early Iron Age we can recognize the first systematic construction of places for ritual purposes, such as the rectangular enclosure at Vix (Chapter 2) and that on the hilltop site at Závist in the Czech Republic. The scale of such constructed sites changed in the fourth and third centuries BC.

The enclosure built at Gournay-sur-Aronde in northern

12. Bronze-covered iron helmet with coral inlay, from Canosa di Puglia in southern Italy. This object, at least part of which was originally covered with gold, exhibits a flamboyant expression of the La Tène style. Height 25 cm.

France represents a new conception of ritual place. Brunaux, the excavator, dates its beginning to the fourth century BC, and it continued in use, with many complex changes to its structure, throughout the Iron Age and into the Gallo-Roman Period. The enclosed space measured 45 by 38 m. There was an entrance at the middle of the east side. The ditches and the pits inside the enclosure were used for the deposition of large quantities of materials, including pottery, weapons and animals, especially cattle. The excavators believe that the Gournay sanctuary was intended to accommodate large numbers of people as participants and for repeated reuse.

The deposition of sizeable sets of metal jewellery, a practice abundantly evident at the end of the Iron Age (Chapter 5), is also well documented from the fourth century BC on. An example is the find from Duchcov, about 80 km northwest of Prague in Bohemia. In the course of repair work at a spring in 1882, workers found a bronze cauldron that contained over 2,500 bronze jewellery items, principally fibulae but including bracelets and other ornaments, all dating to the end of the fourth century BC.

In northern Europe the fourth century BC was also a time of much-increased investment in ritual deposition. At Hjortspring on the island of Als in Denmark, a wooden boat 19 m long with space for 20 oarsmen was deposited in a small pond and weighted down with stones. With the boat was the equipment of a sizeable army, along with the skeletal remains of several animals. Among the objects recovered were 11 iron swords, 169 spears, at least 50 wooden shields and several sets of chain mail. Similar deposits are well known from several centuries later during the Roman Iron Age; the Hjortspring find shows that this tradition began by the fourth century BC.

A different kind of deposit is exemplified by 165 silver vessels recovered at Rogozon in northwest Bulgaria. All are types that were used in ritual activity in the Mediterranean world, 108 bowls, 54 jugs and three beakers. Some of the objects bear inscriptions in Greek that link them directly with ritual, and many have on them scenes of what are thought to be cult activities.

In eastern Europe, the areas around the great kurgans of this time yield abundant evidence of ritual activity, including feasting and the manipulation of symbols important to the group's representation of its identity. At Filippovka, Kurgan 1, nearly 8 m high and in area about 120 x 103 m, was part of a complex of burial mounds near the Ural River. Although the log-built centre of the tomb had been robbed, as at most of the kurgans, excavations in 1987 and 1988 revealed important information about the ceremony of which burial was a part. On the left side of the entrance to the chamber were five stag figurines, each about 50 cm high, made of a wood core covered with gold. On the right of the entrance were four gold-covered iron objects and four gold disks with glass decoration. Just west of the central tomb chamber, two pits were found in the mound that contained objects believed to have been used in the ceremony. In one were three more wooden stag figurines covered with gold and silver, about 42 cm high, and gold ornaments that had been attached to wooden vessels. In the other were nine more gold and silver covered stags, between 40 and 50 cm high, along with vessels and ornaments of gold and silver. These objects were apparently intended to be seen by participants at the funerary ceremony.

The sites of Gournay, Duchcov, Hjortspring, Rogozon and Filippovka are examples of five different kinds of deposition associated with ritual during the fourth century BC. In each instance, the scale of the structures and the character and quantity of objects recovered suggest that these rituals were large public affairs, not the more modest ceremonies of earlier times. As Charlotte Fabech has shown in her studies of ritual in Denmark, such major changes in the character of ritual sites indicate fundamental changes in the ways that societies view themselves.

# 4

# Representations of the Other: First Texts

The first written sources that identify and name peoples of temperate Europe are Greek texts of the sixth and fifth centuries BC. The significance of these texts is not self-evident – we must consider them in light of what we know about Greek concepts of ethnicity and identity at the time. Similarly, later texts that record 'Celtic migrations' and portray a particular type of society as characteristically 'Celtic' need to be understood in terms of Greek and Roman attitudes toward history, tradition and representation of other peoples.

## Context and significance of first naming

The name 'Celt', in the form *Keltoi*, first appears in Greek written sources going back to the sixth century BC, referring to people who inhabited what is now southern France. Credit for the first mentioning of this name usually goes to Hecataeus of Miletus, who used it in reference to groups living around the Greek colony of Massalia. The name also appears in a travel account attributed to Avienus. In the fifth century BC, Herodotus places the Celts in the westernmost parts of Europe, and further notes that the headwaters of the Danube are in their lands.

In the east, Greek observers named the 'Scythians' (*Skythai*) as early as the seventh century BC, first in Asia Minor and slightly later in the lands north of the Black Sea. The groups that the Greeks named Scythians were apparently the same peoples whom early Iranian texts designate as 'Saka' and Assyrian sources call 'Ashguzai'. Greek sources named peoples in other parts of Europe as well, such as Thracians, Illyrians and Iberians, but I shall not attempt to include discussion of them here.

We do not know the origins of the names *Keltoi* and *Skythai*; it is not clear where the Greek writers learned them. While the name *Keltoi* served the purposes of Herodotus and other Greek writers to designate groups in the poorly-known lands of western Europe, all of the peoples so designated surely would not have felt that they belonged to the same group that could be identified with a single name. This important point, with implications for efforts to understand the archaeological evidence in relation to the texts, perhaps can be conveyed best through a more recent, somewhat comparable situation.

When Columbus landed on the island of San Salvador in the Caribbean in 1492, he called the natives he met 'Indians', a name that had nothing to do with they way that the people understood themselves, but reflected his wish to discover a westward route to Asia. This name was universally accepted in Columbus' homeland and throughout Europe, and it came to stand for the indigenous peoples where Columbus first encountered them and throughout all of North and South America. We know that Columbus' use, and the near universal application of this name, failed to take account of the variation in language, religion, economy, social organization, political systems and material culture throughout the Americas. As the archaeology of Early Iron Age Europe indicates, the early Greek use of the name *Keltoi* for the peoples of western Europe similarly misunified many peoples who surely considered themselves different from one another, to judge by the patterning in their material culture (Chapter 2).

Just as the name 'Indian' has become universally embedded in world usage as a result of Columbus' geographically mistaken application of the term, the name 'Celt' became a fixed concept in the minds of Greeks, and later of Romans. The names Gaul and Galatian were applied somewhat later; all three terms had similar meaning, though in some contexts one or the other tended to be used. From these first designations of Celts in the sixth and fifth centuries BC down to the first century AD, the peoples so named occupied an important place in the consciousness of Greek and Roman geographers, thinkers and generals. The earliest references – in Hecataeus, Avienus and Herodotus – do not provide any information about the character of the people; they simply name them and suggest a very general location. (Herodotus describes in some detail the people he calls Scythians.) Only later, from the fourth century BC onwards, do we encounter descriptions, and eventually pictorial representations, of the peoples called Celts. Yet subsequent Greek and Roman commentators, and modern investigators, envision continuity between the sixth-fifth century BC groups and the later Celts and Gauls with whom Greeks and Romans came into regular contact. This linking of the peoples whom the earliest Greek commentators named Celts with later populations designated with the same name created a fixed idea that hindered ancient observers and their modern counterparts from understanding processes of change among the peoples of Iron Age Europe.

## Greek concepts of ethnicity in the sixth and fifth centuries BC

In order to contextualize the early naming of Celts in the west and of Scythians in the east, it is necessary to examine briefly the ways that Greeks conceived of other peoples. What did Hecataeus and Herodotus mean when they used the name

Celts? What was their concept of group identity? In Classical ethnography, ethnic characteristics were thought to co-vary – every member of a group would share the same language, religion, family structure and material culture. But we do not know how inclusive or exclusive Hecataeus and Herodotus intended to be. Did they consider the Celts to be regional groups in southern Gaul, along the Atlantic seaboard and around the headwaters of the Danube? Or did they think that they were widespread across western and central Europe? There is no clue in the texts.

Archaeologists have used Herodotus' assertion to link the peoples around the upper Danube during the fifth century BC with the name Celt. The result has been a general acceptance of the idea that any groups that had material culture of west Hallstatt character (or even all Hallstatt-style material culture) or of early La Tène style were Celts. This procedure is unjustifiable, because Herodotus provides no information about his concept of ethnicity, the basis of his ascription or boundaries between Celts and other groups. The naming in Hecataeus and Herodotus provides no useful information about the identity of Iron Age Europeans. It only tells us about how Greek observers perceived the world north and west of the regions with which they were directly familiar. It tells us that Greeks of the sixth and fifth centuries BC were becoming increasingly aware of non-Greek peoples of Europe and trying to establish categories into which to place them and names to designate them.

At this time – the sixth and fifth centuries BC – the peoples we now know as Greeks were forming their ideas about their own identities as 'Greeks'. This was a process that needs to be examined in the context of specific historical changes in Greece and in neighbouring lands, a project beyond the scope of this book. As Romm points out, before the sixth century BC neither the collective name for Greeks (*Hellenes*) nor that for non-Greeks (*barbaroi*) was used in texts. During the sixth and fifth centuries BC, the peoples we consider Greeks were forming their conceptions of their own collective identity with respect to others. Part of this change in thinking about Greekness in relation to others took place in the context of 'Greek colonization', the establishing of new colonial towns along the coasts of the Mediterranean and Black Seas, a process that brought Greek speakers into increasingly regular interaction with peoples who did not share their language or other aspects of their culture. Hall and others consider the Persian War (480-479 BC) an important event in the formation of Greeks' ideas about their identity with respect to other peoples. This threat to their autonomy caused the city-states, which had regarded one another as different and as enemies, to unite to meet the common foe, in the process creating the concept 'Greek' as a unifying identity. In the context of this war with the Persians, the Greeks first formalized their notion of the 'barbarian' – the person different in significant ways from Greeks. Thus our earliest textual references to Celts and to Scythians date from a time in which the authors and their society were in early stages of conceptualizing differences between themselves and other peoples.

For our purposes here, the principal importance of Hecataeus, Avienus, Herodotus and other Greek authors in their naming of Early Iron Age peoples of Europe was in their creating in the Greek mind names and categories for the peoples west, north, and east of Greece. These concepts – Celt, Scythian and others – were reified and built upon in subsequent centuries. There is no evidence in Early Iron Age Europe to suggest that the indigenous peoples were aware of the Greek designations at this stage, nor that they reacted to them in any way. Later that situation changed.

## Texts and migrations

Greek and Roman texts pertaining to the fourth and third centuries BC, many of which were written centuries later, provide more information about the peoples whom the authors call Celts. It is difficult to know how these peoples were related to those designated Celts by Herodotus and his predecessors, except in the most general sense that all were thought to inhabit western and central parts of Europe. Given analogies in more recent historical circumstances, one cannot help feeling that the Greek and Roman writers were using these names to designate any indigenous individuals or groups from the interior of western and central Europe. There is no compelling evidence to suggest that the Mediterranean observers knew much about the societies north of the Mediterranean shores.

An important act attributed to Celts was the sacking of Rome in 387 BC, an event linked to migrations of people southward across the Alps into northern Italy and associated fighting with Etruscan cities in the Po Plain. The event is recorded in most detail by the Roman historian Livy, writing nearly four centuries afterwards. Such an account, with its considerable dramatic detail, we need to regard as a literary product created to convey themes important to Roman tradition and sense of self. Livy's purpose in writing was largely to teach his audience about how Rome came to be as it was at the time of his writing, in the first century BC. There is little doubt that the event took place, but Livy's account surely contains imaginative embellishment. The essence of Livy's story is that Rome was vulnerable, dangerous enemies lurked in the north and only the maintenance of traditional Roman values could save the city in its times of greatest need. These messages were probably tailored to requirements of the Augustan world of the last decades BC.

Polybius, writing during the second century BC, and Pliny in the middle of the first century AD, also describe migrations of

Celts from north of the Alps into Italy. Polybius provides considerable detail about the nature of the society of the Cisalpine Gauls, and many modern reconstructions of Celtic life are based on his descriptions. Such generalization is problematic for several reasons. First, in his accounts of the Celts of northern Italy, Polybius, though he spent time in Italy, was still an outsider to the peoples he describes. Secondly, despite much focused investigation, archaeology does not indicate transplantation of peoples from north of the Alps into northern Italy on a scale that would accord with the textual tradition about migrations. It is more likely that movement across the Alps took place sporadically over centuries, as discussion of mobility above in Chapters 2 and 3 would suggest. In some instances, larger movements may have caught the attention of commentators in Italy, and they may have recorded them as mass migrations. But the archaeology does not support any movement on such a scale. Instead, the material evidence can be best understood in terms of the spread of the new La Tène style discussed in Chapter 3 – some movement of people surely took place, as was common during the Iron Age, but the more important mechanism was probably enthusiasm on the part of indigenous groups for adopting the new stylistic fashion.

Numerous texts document the hiring of Celtic mercenaries between the fourth and second centuries BC for service in armies of potentates in Mediterranean lands. We read of Celtic mercenaries fighting in Greece in 369-368 BC and shortly after serving in Sicily. In 307 BC, Celtic warriors are mentioned participating in an invasion of Carthaginian north Africa. In the early third century BC, they are mentioned increasingly in Hellenistic armies serving in the aid of local potentates competing for power after the death of Alexander the Great. One contingent of Celtic troops was sent to Egypt to participate in a dynastic conflict in 277-276 BC. Celtic warriors gained a reputation for courage and ferocity, and their services were much in demand. Greek texts mention Celtic warrior bands in south-eastern Europe and in Asia Minor. In 279 BC one is said to have sacked the sanctuary complex at Delphi. Actions by such raiding parties and the service of mercenaries in Greek armies were probably not always sharply distinguished by commentators.

As with the texts pertaining to Celtic migrations into Italy, these sources about Celtic mercenaries and warrior bands are also problematic. The writers do not explain what they mean by Celtic in reference to the hired warriors. As in the case of Herodotus, it is most likely that with that term they meant simply soldiers from western and central Europe. However imprecisely these textual representations portray the fighters whom they designate as Celts, they are important sources of information in indicating mechanisms through which Iron Age Europeans became knowledgeable about larger-scale societies of the Mediterranean world. The growing familiarity of people throughout Europe with Italy, Greece, even Egypt and Carthaginian north Africa – whether through personal experience as mercenaries or through hearing stories told by returning warriors – made them increasingly aware that, as peoples of Iron Age Europe, they shared a way of life, material culture and belief system that distinguished them from the peoples to the south. We should expect to see in the archaeological evidence in temperate Europe indicators of changes in identity as the result of such new knowledge.

A large proportion of men who served as mercenaries probably returned to their homelands. I would predict two kinds of responses. Like all travellers, some would have brought home objects acquired abroad, and they might adopt practices they witnessed. At the same time, they would have been likely to reformulate their feelings about their identities with respect to the wider social world with which they had been confronted.

The earliest more detailed descriptions of the peoples called Celts by Greek and Roman writers begin in the fourth century

BC, and they often dwell on their bellicose nature. As a result, we often read in modern treatments of the Celts that they were a warlike people, quick to join combat. But of course, most of these texts derive from contexts of warfare – Greek and later Roman writers recording military exploits of these groups in Italy and in southeast Europe. Not until the time of Caesar in the 50s BC do we encounter a description of the peoples of interior Europe in their homelands; then too, we are dealing with a military man's account of groups he was attacking. The stereotype of Celts as warlike people needs to be discarded.

The same limited perspective and bias applies to pictorial representations of Celts. The earliest portrayal of Celts may be on a ceramic *stamnos* from southern Etruria in Italy, dated 400-375 BC, showing a battle scene, thought to represent Celts fighting Italic peoples. Other early depictions said to represent Celts are similarly military in nature, such as gravestones at Bologna, relief sculptures at Pergamum and several familiar statues of wounded warriors, including that known as the Dying Gaul. In some cases, the figures are represented with objects that may link them with homelands north of the Alps, such as the torc around the neck of the Dying Gaul and shields with some of the warriors, but there is no reason to think that these were more than stereotypical emblems that marked these figures as barbarian Celts in the minds of the sculptors and their audiences.

### Who were the Greeks' Celts?

Much has been written about the La Tène style and its association with Celts. Popular accounts and much scholarly writing connect the two. Yet given the way the name Celt was used by Greek writers of the sixth and fifth centuries BC, there is no basis to the assertion that La Tène style is associated with Celts. The name Celt and the ornamental style created in the fifth century BC are two different categories of information that are not necessarily directly connected.

Malcolm Chapman has argued the position that the Greek and Roman texts are too problematic for us to base any detailed assessments of identity upon them. The principal problem is that we do not know what Hecataeus, Herodotus, Polybius, Caesar or any of the other writers meant when they wrote that a group was Celtic – we do not know their criteria for ascribing identity. Nor do we know what other categories those writers may have had in mind to which they were opposing the designation Celt. There is good reason to think that for many Greek and Roman observers, Celt and Gaul simply meant 'barbarian from the north'. Given this lack of specificity, trying to link particular archaeological assemblages with a name such as 'Celt' is not only fruitless but misguided.

For the early phases of Greek use of the name Celt, I agree with this position. But over time, as Greeks used the concept and the name Celt, and as Iron Age Europeans interacted in a variety of contexts with Mediterranean peoples, through migration, mercenary service and trade, some Iron Age peoples surely became familiar with and adopted the name Celt as their own. This process is well documented ethnohistorically in many contexts. Our challenge is to recognize when this Greek name – and perhaps some of the characteristics ascribed to Celts – were adopted by some of the peoples so designated, and to examine what role that adoption played in constructing their self-perception and guiding their interactions with others.

# 5

# Territoriality and Identity in the Late Iron Age Landscape

This chapter examines widespread changes in the ways that communities defined and expressed their identities during the final two centuries BC, apparent in a new emphasis on creating bounded settlements and new practices of deposition. Funerary ritual changed over much of Europe, with a decline in individual burial in favour of communal mortuary practices. A similar shift in emphasis from identity of the individual to identity of the community is apparent in patterns of manufacture of everyday objects and in the emergence of coinage.

During this period, Rome was in the process of its imperial expansion, with increasing political and military activity in Iberia, southern Gaul, northern Italy and the east Alpine region. In response to the ever greater entanglement of Rome in European political and economic affairs, Iron Age peoples joined together in new ways to establish and communicate their corporate identities. Much of the archaeological evidence for increased importance of regional and interregional identification can be understood in this context of response to Rome's imperial ambitions and actions.

## Creating new boundaries

During the second century BC, communities throughout the central regions of the continent constructed walled settlements on a scale vastly larger than any earlier sites in temperate Europe (Figure 13). As many as 150 such sites have been identified, all characterized by massive walls built of earth, stone facing and timber and situated in topographic locations offering natural defensive advantages. The creation of these fortified settlements, known as *oppida* after Julius Caesar's use of that term, was a fundamental change in the organization of space. For this part of Europe, what had been a landscape of open villages consisting of timber-frame houses, more or less evenly distributed across central regions of the continent, was transformed into one differentiated into large enclosed settlement spaces and many more, much smaller, unenclosed settlements. Some *oppida*, such as Bibracte, Manching and Stradonice, became densely inhabited centres of manufacturing and commerce, with populations in the several thousands. Others, such as Kelheim and Závist, yield evidence of more modest occupation. A few, such as Zarten, appear to have remained largely unoccupied, perhaps intended for use in time of emergency only. No common pattern is evident in the internal organization of these sites, but rather considerable local variability. However, the creation of large enclosed areas and the architecture of the walls indicate that similar changes were taking place all over temperate Europe. The Late Iron Age *oppida*, ranging in size between about 10 and 500 hectares, were much larger than Early Iron Age enclosed towns such as Mont Lassois and the Heuneburg. The *oppidum* walls were the largest human-built structures in the landscape of pre-Roman Europe, and they had an importance far beyond a strictly military purpose.

The principal significance of the *oppida* for our concerns here is in the definition of central, highly fortified settlement areas in a landscape that had been relatively undifferentiated. Construction of the walls around these settlements was a major investment of labour and resources. Whatever the original

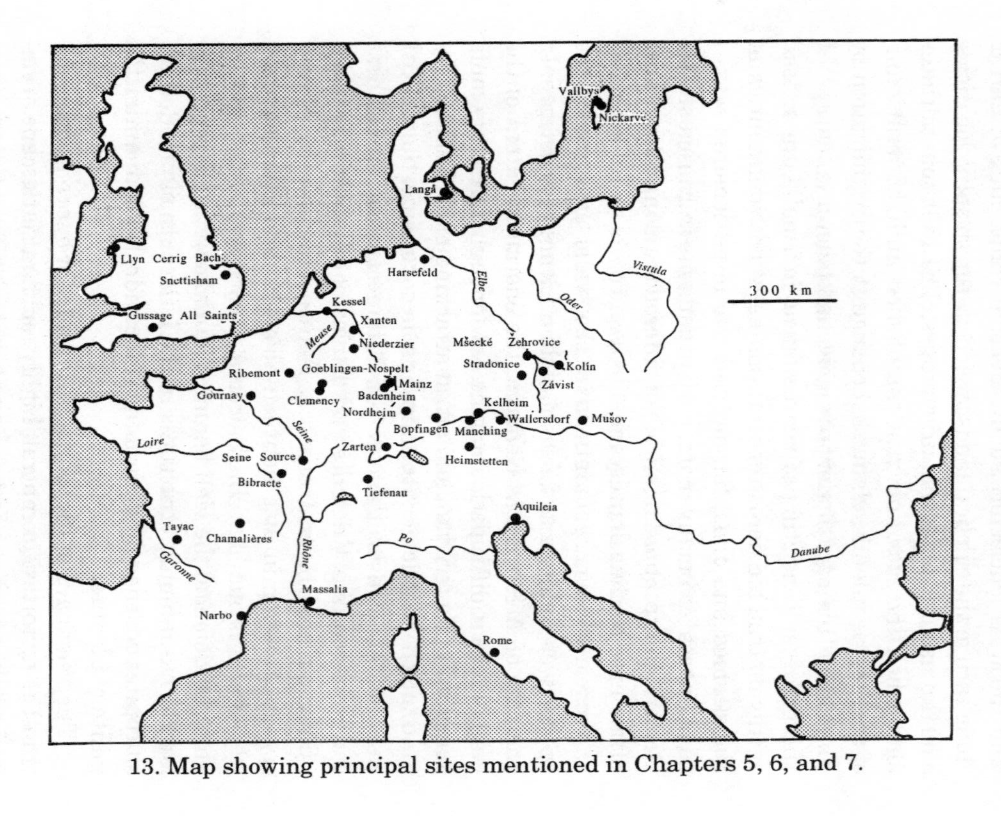


13. Map showing principal sites mentioned in Chapters 5, 6, and 7.

purpose of the *oppida* and their walls (there is considerable discussion about these issues), the much larger communities and the walls enclosing them served to create a new kind of difference in the cultural landscape, between those living inside and those outside. Recent survey research at Kelheim indicates that when the *oppidum* was established and the walls constructed, people from small communities in the vicinity abandoned their settlements to move into the new centre. Yet the great majority of people remained in small, unenclosed settlements. This new differentation between communities at the centres and those at outlying rural settlements was a fundamental departure from earlier patterns in European settlement and created a new kind of difference among inhabitants of the Late Iron Age landscape.

Some investigators argue that the walls at some of the *oppida* were built more for display than for military defence. In the case of sites such as Kelheim, the enormous extent of the walls make it difficult to imagine how enough defenders could have been mustered to hold off an attacking enemy effectively, since neither settlement remains inside nor sites in the vicinity outside the walls suggest a population of great size. These purposes – military defence and display of community identity – need not have been mutually exclusive. A town wall is always a sign of a community's identity and of the distinction between it and others outside. When a community erects a wall specifically for defence, the wall becomes much more than a military barrier. As a highly visible structure in the cultural landscape, it creates a sense of separateness and adds to a community's sense of identity.

The rectangular enclosures known as *Viereckschanzen* are another important component of the cultural landscape. Typically defined by a surrounding V-shaped ditch and an inner wall, they measure around 90 by 90 m, though dimensions vary. Many hundreds have been identified, and more are recognized every year, especially through aerial observation. Results of numerous recent excavations, especially in southern Germany, challenge the long-accepted view that these were places created specifically for ritual. Recent work at Bopfingen and Nordheim, for example, has yielded abundant evidence for domestic activity, including pottery of different kinds, animal bones, metal objects and daub. The fact that very few other settlements are known from this period besides the *oppida* supports the idea that most of the enclosures were probably parts of settlements. At Nordheim investigators found that a palisade stood on top of the wall, contributing to the idea of a defensive function of the enclosures.

Yet many of the investigated enclosures yield evidence for activity that corresponds to what we think of as ritual. In northern France, enclosures at Gournay-sur-Aronde and Ribemont, with their extensive deposits of damaged weapons, animal bones and human bones, reflect activity that was not just domestic in the sense of household economic activity. The large wooden figures from the bottom of the shaft at Fellbach-Schmiden suggest some kind of ritual activity, as does the carved limestone head associated with the enclosure at Mšecké Žehrovice in Bohemia. The excavations at Nordheim revealed a deposit that contained a Roman amphora and eight iron shield bosses, not a usual settlement deposit.

Recent research in Iron Age Britain offers ways of reconciling these apparently contradictory aspects of the enclosures. Barry Cunliffe at Danebury and more generally J.D. Hill have shown that many excavated settlements include evidence from activity that was not directly part of what we consider domestic, but rather belongs to the category we call ritual. These studies challenge our traditional division of past human activity into categories such as 'settlement', 'burial' and 'ritual' and make us realize that Iron Age Europeans probably thought about their world in ways that are not familiar to us. Archaeologists have long distinguished between settlement and ritual behaviour, but this distinction may not be relevant to the way Iron Age peoples understood their daily lives. The evidence now seems to indicate that most of the enclosures served as protection for farmsteads, but that in addition to what we consider usual habitation activities, people used their material culture in rituals that involved such actions as depositing weapons in pits, wooden figural sculptures in wells and stone heads near enclosures. But among the many hundreds of enclosures in the landscape of temperate Europe, we must allow for variability in the ways people used them.

Both typology and radiocarbon determinations show that the enclosures were contemporaneous with the *oppida*. We can understand them as results of the response of a portion of the rural population to the same circumstances that stimulated the creation of the *oppida*. One aspect of this response was greater need for defence – hence the ditch, wall, and palisade; but another was the demarcation of interior community space from exterior open areas. As with the *oppida*, these enclosures can be understood both as a result of a perceived need on the part of people, and as a cause of further feelings about division, separation and territoriality. While the enclosures have been identified throughout all of the central regions of Europe where the *oppida* exist, they are highly concentrated in southern Germany. This distribution was long thought to be a result of differential research intensity, but now that research on these sites has increased greatly in the past 20 years, this concentration is still evident. Apparently in some regions – particularly Germany south of the Danube, Late Iron Age communities frequently chose to build these structures for their rural settlements, while in other regions, such as eastern France, they more often chose unenclosed arrangements. In the choices involving these settlement forms we can see differences in the decisions that people made. The results of those decisions –

enclosed versus unenclosed rural settlements – in turn created different kinds of social environments.

## New patterns of deposition

During the second century BC, funerary practice changed in most of the central regions of temperate Europe. Cremation gradually replaced inhumation as the dominant burial practice, and in most areas where *oppida* existed, subsurface burial was largely abandoned. Funerary practices following this change are not well understood, because their final stage no longer included graves. What we find instead is evidence for the deposition of sizeable quantities of human bone on some settlements, such as Manching, and in other contexts, such as at enclosures in northern France and in the River Meuse at Kessel in the Netherlands. At the same time, metal tools and weapons were deposited at both watery and dry-land places.

The bone deposits have been interpreted to indicate practices such as exhumation and manipulation of human skeletal material in funerary rituals. In northern France, excavations at Gournay-sur-Aronde, Ribemont and Mirebeau have yielded large quantities of human bone, in some cases clearly selected and arranged by skeletal part, indicating a new practice very different in character from earlier rituals that involved the creation of individual burial structures and assemblages.

In other cases, deposits of human bones occur on settlements. At Manching, remains of well over 400 individuals have been recovered and analysed. Similar deposits of human bones have been identified at other settlements, including Bad Nauheim, Breisach-Hochstetten, Basel-Gasfabrik and Knovíze. Analyses of the Manching bones, recovered principally in postholes, pits and ditches, show that they had been selected systematically. Femurs, humuri, tibiae and skulls are the most common, while ribs, vertebrae and extremities are rare. Fragments of skulls are often associated with iron swords in pits. Skull and longbone fragments indicate that many bones were broken intentionally after death. Many longbones show cut marks that Hahn interprets as resulting from cutting away the flesh with knives, probably part of the ritual. (He excludes cannibalism as the principal reason for the presence of these bones and of the cut marks on them.) Comparison of the Manching skeletal materials with those from Gournay and Ribemont reveals similar patterns in breakage and cut marks.

At Ribemont, the arrangement of bones suggests the collection and deposition of remains of large numbers of individuals in a central place. At Manching, on the other hand, the bone remains are scattered broadly over much of the settlement area. Hahn suggests that this pattern is related directly to the organization of the settlement, with distinct family units inhabiting different parts of the settlement area.

The shift away from the practice of inhumation with grave goods that characterized funerary behaviour during the preceding centuries can be understood in terms of changing emphases, away from the individual as a distinct entity, given his/her own, separate burial place with distinctive grave goods. The bone deposits at Manching and other settlements suggest rituals that emphasized the community rather than the individual.

While the change in predominant funerary practice meant that large quantities of material wealth, especially in metalwork, were no longer being placed in graves, there was new emphasis on depositing metalwork in pits in the ground and in bodies of water. A few examples illustrate the character of some different deposits. A hoard of iron tools found in a pit at Kolín in Bohemia contained 68 objects, all different and representing a variety of activities, including agriculture, iron smithing and food preparation. At Tiefenau in Switzerland, a deposit of about a thousand objects contained iron swords, all bent or broken and sometimes with bronze scabbards, horse harness and chariot fittings and coins. From a dried-up lake-bed at Llyn Cerrig Bach in Wales were recovered swords, spearheads, an ornate bronze shield boss, bridle parts, chariot fittings, a bronze trumpet and a pair of cauldrons. Deposits at Niederzier in the lower Rhineland (Figure 14), Saint-Louis in Alsace and Tayac in southwestern France contained gold neck rings and gold coins. Others, such as at Wallersdorf in Bavaria, include hundreds of newly minted gold coins. A ditched enclosure at Snettisham in East Anglia contained at least eleven separate deposits of gold, silver and bronze, in the form of neck rings, bracelets, coins and bars, totalling some 40 kg of metal. In foothill regions of the Alps, quantities of metal objects and animal parts were deposited in the process of fire rituals that have been identified at many sites.

14. Gold objects from a hoard recovered at Niederzier, west of Cologne, Germany, in the course of excavations in 1978. The three rings are made of sheet gold; with them were 46 gold coins.

Common to the hundreds of known deposits of which these are examples are objects of special meaning, workmanship and value. In most cases, we lack information about the practices that preceded the deposition of the objects. The settings – mostly in open, exposed places – as well as the quantities of material involved, strongly suggest that the ceremonies of which these deposits were part were public displays rather than private offerings.

## Material culture and community

This same shift in emphasis from the individual to the community can be recognized in patterns of manufacturing. For the first time, the majority of the pottery, at least at the *oppida*, was mass produced on the potter's wheel, not individually crafted. Much larger quantities of iron tools were manufactured than ever before, also in series production. Most striking is a shift in the character of personal ornaments, especially fibulae.

In the Early Iron Age and the early and middle phases of the Late Iron Age, fibulae were individually crafted, and many were unique. Many fibulae in the flat grave cemeteries of the fourth and third centuries BC have ornate cast bows, and some have inlay of coral or enamel, requiring considerable investment of time and effort in making the objects. In this final phase of the Iron Age, the most common fibula in the central regions of the continent was the Nauheim type, a simple forged fibula with a minimum of individual variation. Experiments by Drescher and by Furger-Gunti show that the Nauheim fibula was ideally suited to mass production. Thus in personal ornaments we can identify a fundamental shift from fibulae that were intended to express individuality to fibulae that offered little choice for individual display.

Organization of the manufacture of personal ornaments is not well understood, but it was apparently dispersed. Some *oppida* were sites of intensive production, but some small communities practised iron and bronze working as well, and even minted coins. At the otherwise typical farmstead at Gussage All Saints in southern Britain, excavators found abundant evidence for casting bronze chariot ornaments and harness attachments, including over 7,000 fragments of moulds, along with furnace remains and sherds of crucibles. This small community apparently was producing goods for elite warriors. Small communities such as Gussage were tightly integrated into the emerging systems of regional political power, and the individuals who made the ornaments must have identified with a larger entity.

Changes in coinage also point to transformations in patterns of regional identity. Gold coinage first appeared in temperate Europe during the third century BC, in the context of returning mercenaries who brought with them gold coins from the Greek world. During the second century BC both silver and bronze coins came into use in continental Europe. Coins provide important information about group identities at the time of the changes at the end of the second and start of the first centuries BC. The communities at many *oppida* minted coins, and some at small unenclosed settlements did as well; the majority of coins were distinctive of the place where they were minted. While coins circulated throughout Europe and provide information about mobility and trade, most are recovered within a 75 km radius of their place of origin. Like their Roman (and modern) counterparts, coins served both as tokens of standard value and as signs of identity among territorial groups.

From the final quarter of the second century BC to the middle of the final century BC, many coins bear legends in Latin or Greek characters. Most often these are personal names, probably of the individuals who controlled the mints. The use of legends represents the earliest adoption of writing in many of these areas, and as such constitutes important information about borrowing means of communicating identity from the literate Mediterranean societies. During the final quarter of the second and first half of the final century BC, coins became much more abundant than before, and specific types appear to conform to particular territories, possibly to individual tribes (see below). When people used coins minted by the leaders of their communities, with images and names that identified those individuals and motifs significant to the group, the association must have played an important role in strengthening the person's sense of belonging to that community.

The creation of new bounded settlements, the change from individual burial to communal bone deposition, the proliferation of large offerings made in open places and the development of mass-produced goods, all signal a shift away from the material expression of individual identity and toward the expression of the identity of the community. These changes were complex, they happened at different rates and in different ways, and it is difficult to know the extent to which they were perceived by the people who experienced them. Only with the advantage of being able to look back at the material evidence from across Europe during these two centuries is it possible to see the broad outline of this transformation. This fundamental change took place in the context of the economic, political and military expansion of Rome.

## Roman expansion and territorial identity

Rome's victories over Carthage during the second half of the third century BC, its expansion in Italy and its annexation of provinces along the shores of the east and central Mediterranean, gained Rome vast economic resources, political power and military might and brought Roman establishments close to routes into the interior of Europe. Rome founded the trade port of Aquileia at the head of the Adriatic in 181 BC and conquered the Po Plain in northern Italy by around 180 BC; these advances provided easier access northward through the Alpine passes. In southern Gaul, textual sources attest to Roman military intervention on behalf of the city of Massalia in 181, 154, and 125 BC. Those episodes culminated in the establishment of a colony at Narbo in 118 BC, a base for diplomatic envoys and merchants on the Mediterranean coast not far from the mouth of the Rhône and that corridor northward into the interior of the continent. Commerce throughout the Mediterranean basin expanded rapidly during the second and first centuries BC.

Signs of growing interaction with the Mediterranean world appear in temperate Europe from the start of the second century BC, including amphorae, bronze vessels, fine pottery, implements of various kinds and coins. The formation of the *oppida*, changes in funerary practices, expansion of ritual deposition and creation of territorially distinctive coinages can be understood in the context of the Europe-wide changes that included Roman expansion and intensified commerce throughout the Mediterranean region. The mechanisms of change are not clear, but a number of factors can be noted. The great expansion of commerce in the Mediterranean basin during the second century BC had a number of important effects in temperate Europe. It stimulated production of goods sought by Mediterranean societies, including agricultural and forest products, metals and probably slaves. The increased circulation of goods, and the growth in material wealth that resulted, may have played a role in stimulating some of the migrations from northern and eastern parts of Europe into southern temperate Europe between 120 and 60 BC recorded in the texts. Defence against migrating bands was one factor in the emergence of the *oppida*. In addition, the intensified production favoured the concentration of manufacturing and commerce at central locations, which grew in population. This concentration of economic activity and of population at many of the *oppida* contributed to increasing identification of individuals with the regional centre into which they moved or with which they became more tightly linked through production for trade with Roman merchants. Returning mercenary soldiers probably played roles in both the growing mobile violence and the increase in manufacturing and commerce.

A number of burials west of the Rhine provides insight into these changes. Though subsurface burial declined during the second century BC in much of temperate Europe (see above), between the middle and lower Rhine and the English Channel the practice continued, and outfitting some graves with lavish assemblages of objects was resumed. Characteristic are material paraphernalia of complex funeral feasts that included Roman luxury goods such as bronze vessels and fine pottery, sometimes accompanied by the amphorae that carried wine; and traditional signs of status and power in Europe, such as wheeled vehicles, horse-riding equipment and ornate weapons. A burial at Clemency in Luxembourg, dated at around 70 BC, contained a large assemblage of implements for a feast, many of Mediterranean provenance. These included at least ten ceramic amphorae of Roman manufacture, an iron brazier, 27 ceramic vessels of local character, remains of four pigs, a bronze cauldron and an oil lamp, as well as elaborate textiles and personal ornaments of metal. A significant detail is the observation by the excavators that the majority of the Roman amphorae had been intentionally smashed before deposition, a practice documented later in the burials at Goeblingen-Nospelt.

Four richly outfitted burials at Goeblingen-Nospelt in Luxembourg illustrate the process through which elite individuals reconfigured their identities following the Roman conquest. All four were enclosed, together with a number of modest burials, within a rectangular space about 61 by 34 m, defined by a ditch. All contained cremations, placed inside wooden burial chambers and covered with mounds. Two graves, C and D, are dated to the first two decades after the conquest, 50-30 BC. The other two are later, Grave A about 25 BC and B about 20 BC. Two processes of change are particularly noteworthy in this series. One is the progressive increase over time in quantities of distinctively Roman objects, the other is the steadfast maintenance of local burial traditions.

The earliest of the four, C, had no Roman-made objects. The latest, B, contained an elaborate set of Roman fine ceramic tableware, bronze wine-service vessels and a lamp, indicating not just the adoption of Roman objects, but of meaningfully-constituted sets intended for specific ritual purposes. Yet this grave also contained a local long sword with a scabbard decorated in traditional fashion, spurs and other horse-riding equipment and local ceramic and metal vessels. Roman practice did not include burying weapons in graves, nor elaborate sets of feasting equipment. The presence of these assemblages expresses forcefully that the buried individuals, and by implication the communities of which they were part, viewed themselves principally in terms of their traditional backgrounds. They adopted what they chose from the Roman world (amphorae and the liquids they contained, bronze vessels, ceramic tableware, lamp) but contextualized that material in their own milieu (by including it in a grave, and by integrating it into local sets of feasting equipment). The spurs may signal service in the Roman army as cavalry (see below), and the full set of Roman tableware is probably indicative of the adopting of Roman banqueting practices. But the entire assemblage was integrated into the context of elite burial tradition in temperate Europe. These rich graves at Goeblingen-Nospelt show the recreation of burial practice from several centuries before in the structuring of identity in the context of newly-conquered Gaul.

The expansion of Roman political and economic activities during the second and first centuries BC had a major impact on these patterns in temperate Europe. The burials at Clemency and Goeblingen-Nospelt exemplify processes of reaction to the increasing effects of Roman expansion. As those effects became increasingly felt throughout Gaul, local leaders rose in status and power as communities felt threatened by that expansion. To communicate the identity of their elites in this context of contention and stress, communities reached back to earlier traditions of burial ritual for practices that asserted their identities as non-Romans, reconstituting the use of mounds, wooden chambers and large sets of feasting paraphernalia in the graves. These efforts at reasserting traditional local identities increased at the same time that the *oppida* were established, their great boundary walls constructed and bronze and silver, as well as gold, coinage was coming into use. All of these changes point to an ever-stronger identification of the individual and the community with a particular territory.

The establishment of new places of ritual deposition further attests to this intensifying identification with territory. Both the source of the Seine in eastern France and Chamalières in the Massif Central were places at which people arranged carved wooden figures associated with worship at a spring. About 300 figures have been recovered at the source of the Seine, about 5,000 at Chamalières. In addition to the wooden figures, which combine elements of indigenous costume and personal ornament with styles of the early Roman Period, an inscribed lead tablet was recovered at Chamalières bearing some 60 words in Gaulish language and Italic letters, evoking indigenous deities. The text both affirms the interpretation of the site as a place of votive offering and demonstrates the complex intermingling of indigenous and Roman traditions. At the sanctuary at Bolards at Nuits-Saint-Georges in the Côte-d'Or, several hundred deposited fibulae attest to the ritual use of a spring beginning shortly after the conquest; later an elaborate Gallo-Roman ritual complex was constructed on the site.

These graves and ritual sites show that in the areas conquered by the Roman army, there was highly complex negotiation of local identities in conjunction with transformations introduced by the Roman presence. An important subject for future research is the situation of such graves and deposits with respect to centres and boundaries of territories of the emerging regional groups.

## Interregional identities

Throughout the final century BC, a new degree of uniformity in material culture is apparent throughout temperate Europe, even during the disruptions created by the Roman military campaigns in Gaul. Across what had been a stylistic frontier between the regions in which the La Tène style was predominant and those to the north in which the Jastorf tradition flourished, and also across the Roman frontier established by Caesar at the Rhine, types of personal ornaments, of bronze vessels and of burials demonstrate a common identity that challenges the notion of the divisions implied by the political frontiers. Völling's studies of fibulae and belt hooks illustrate these new patterns. In place of the strongly regional distributions during the preceding centuries, the new types are widely represented on both sides of the supposed frontiers.

In southern central Europe, where subsurface burial had gone out of fashion during the second century BC, the practice was revived around the middle of the final century BC, about the time of Caesar's campaigns in Gaul when many of the *oppida* east of the Rhine were abandoned. I have argued elsewhere that these graves reflect characteristic responses by communities to the collapse of the political and economic systems centred at the *oppida*. Unlike burials of the fourth, third and first half of the second centuries BC, these graves show diverse funerary rites and grave goods. Some contained inhumations, others cremations. Objects placed in the graves included fibulae, belt hooks and pottery, some similar to objects at the *oppida*, others – particularly fibulae and belt hooks – of wider pan-European character.

We can understand the funerary rituals reflected in these graves as responses to the disruptive effects of the Roman military ventures west of the Rhine and the collapse of the *oppida* east of it. As the economic and social systems of which the *oppida* were part broke down, people moved out to establish new communities and, at a time of considerable cultural stress, sought to recreate identities based in part on past traditions and in part on borrowing and adapting traditions from neighbouring peoples. On the one hand they were reaching back in time using historical memory to recreate the practices of the past – before the abandonment of the subsurface burial practice around the mid-second century BC. On the other hand, they were embracing the increasingly cosmopolitan, Europe-wide signs of greater mobility and unity among indigenous peoples throughout the continent. Each of the graves of this context is distinctly different from the others in terms of ritual and grave goods.

In the regions east of the middle and lower Rhine, the burying of weapons in men's graves first became regular practice around the time of the Roman military campaigns in Gaul. For the first time in these regions, men were being identified in the funerary ceremony as warriors. We can understand this development in the context of heightened military activity that accompanied Roman expansion into temperate Europe. During his campaigns in Gaul, Caesar crossed the Rhine on at least two occasions, directly threatening the peoples east of the river. Caesar informs us in his commentary that he made use in the Gallic campaigns of Germans as auxiliary troops. Surely the decade of fighting in Gaul that resulted from the Roman incursions made all the peoples east of the Rhine aware of the importance of military preparedness. These developments led to a new emphasis on military themes east of the Rhine and to growing identification of men as warriors, a change well represented in the rapid proliferation of graves with weapons.

Together with this new emphasis on the identity of men as warriors east of the Rhine from around the middle of the final century BC, was the appearance of a widespread new identity that has been called the 'international warrior elite'. A large number of well-outfitted men's burials from the middle of the final century BC onwards, characterized by long iron swords, scabbards often ornamented in openwork patterns, lances, shields, spurs, sometimes helmets, bronze vessels and sometimes wagons, have been identified on both sides of the Rhine and as far north as central Scandinavia. The appearance of similar burial assemblages over much of Europe, distinguished by weapons, horse gear and luxuries, suggests that a particular elite identity was forming that linked different regional populations on a larger scale, even across the Roman frontier. The weapons and general wealth of these graves indicates a strong indigenous component to this new identity, yet the presence of spurs and Roman imports links it to Rome. Spurs, when they are present, may relate directly to the role these individuals played as cavalry troops in Roman service (see below).

Examples of these international warrior elite graves include several that contain swords and other weapons together with spurs and Roman bronze vessels in the large cemetery of Harsefeld on the lower Elbe. A rich cremation grave at Langå on the island of Fyn in Denmark belongs to this group. Objects in the burial included four swords, a spearhead and a shield, two gold finger rings, a four-wheeled wagon and two bronze vessels, one from Italy and one from southern temperate Europe. Further north, on the island of Gotland, graves at Nickarve and Vallbys contained complete sets of weapons – swords, spears and shields, and in each instance a single spur – linking these individuals with their counterparts on the continent to the south.

# 6

# Outsiders' Views: Roman and Greek Representations

The most abundant source of written information about Iron Age Europeans concerns the final two centuries BC. As a result of diverse interactions between peoples in temperate Europe and societies of the Mediterranean world over the preceding centuries, the groups were acquiring knowledge about one another, and the process of learning had important effects on identity formation and on representation of the other. Critical reading of the texts, informed by recent scholarship on written and pictorial representations of others in different historical contexts, helps us to understand the relationship between these Greek and Roman texts and the Iron Age peoples they were portraying.

## Accumulating results of entanglements

From the final two centuries BC we have much richer written information in Greek and Roman authors about the Iron Age peoples of Europe than ever before. It is of a different character, for several reasons. By the second century BC many peoples in temperate Europe had been in direct contact with communities in the Mediterranean world, through mercenary service, trade, political interactions and other mechanisms. Some authors, such as Julius Caesar, were directly familiar with the Iron Age Europeans about whom they wrote.

The extensive interactions between members of communities north of the Alps and groups in the Mediterranean basin during the fourth, third and second centuries BC provided ample opportunity for members of both groups to become familiar with members of the other and to form ideas about them. In the process, all those involved continuously recreated their own identities in response to the changing situations around them.

To help us to understand how these complex processes worked, it is helpful to examine better documented situations in comparable contexts elsewhere in time and space. Much recent research focuses on interactions in the context of European exploration, conquest and colonization of different parts of the Americas (Chapter 4). In many instances in the New World, native groups assumed, in part, identities ascribed *to* them by Europeans. In the Iron Age, the groups who lived north and west of the Alps in the fifth century BC when Herodotus was writing almost certainly did not consider themselves Celts. But by the second century BC, as a result of many different kinds of interactions that had taken place between the peoples of temperate Europe and Mediterranean societies, many surely must have been familiar with the names *Keltoi* and *Galli* that the Greeks and the Romans used to designate them. In this sense, the Greeks and Romans created the Celts/ Gauls, just as Columbus created the Indians of the Americas – the category 'Indian' had meaning to Columbus and other Europeans, but not to the indigenous peoples of the Americas. In both instances, through interaction with the more complex societies, the indigenous peoples came to adopt these categories. By the final century BC there most likely were Celts/ Gauls north of the Alps, according to both the outsiders' and the insiders' understandings.

In modern instances, it is clear that indigenous peoples also have a strong impact on the ways that groups that move into their lands perceive themselves. Effects of interaction with Native American peoples on the Europeans settling in the

Americas are extensively documented, as is the impact on the self-understanding of the nineteenth-century British of their colonial interactions with the peoples of India. Similarly, in the varied processes of interaction from the sixth century BC onwards, the Iron Age peoples of temperate Europe must have had important effects on the ways that Greeks and Romans restructured their own ideas about themselves and about others. This important topic is beyond the scope of our discussion here.

## Texts as cultural constructions: representations of Iron Age peoples

Instead of accepting the texts by Greek and Roman commentators as statements of historical fact, we must, of course, understand them as cultural constructions. Different observers note and record different information. Each text is just one of multiple possible perspectives on the peoples and events it represents. The implications are apparent in a comparison of two contemporaneous accounts by different observers of a single indigenous group, such as Johann Georg Kohl's and Henry Schoolcraft's different ethnographies of the Lake Superior Ojibway in the mid-nineteenth century. Unfortunately, in the case of Greek and Roman texts about the indigenous peoples of Europe, we rarely have access to different perspectives, until the time of the Roman Empire. (Caesar, Strabo, Tacitus and Cassius Dio provide divergent representations of the Celt-German distinction – see below.) Usually one source survives about any particular topic. In cases for which we have several accounts, frequently all can be traced back to a single original source. Each representation of a group by an outside observer is of necessity based on a single experience or set of experiences, under particular circumstances of which the reader is often not aware. Just as the patterning in the material evidence does not speak for itself – we must have a theory in the context of which to understand the evidence, so too the ancient texts do not speak for themselves – we need critically-developed theories and methods for dealing with them in order to make them meaningful.

The issue of source criticism is particularly complex in relation to the Greek and Roman texts about indigenous Iron Age Europeans. The meaning of the information preserved in a text depends upon a variety of factors. One is the ways that an author gathered the information. We know that Caesar obtained his information about the Gauls in part through his own direct observations and in part from local informants. Tacitus gathered his data largely through research in archives in Rome. Livy, writing in Rome around the time of Christ, based most of his accounts of the Gallic migrations into Italy during the fifth and fourth centuries BC on Roman oral tradition, a kind of memory-keeping that is more fluid and flexible than written documents. Herodotus was never at the headwaters of the Danube, and he collected his information about that region from people he met during his travels in the eastern and central Mediterranean. Another factor is the author's world view. How did these writers view the world and their place in it? What was the author's intention in communicating with his audience? Herodotus' concerns in writing his accounts of the Scythians were different from Livy's purposes in recording centuries-old Roman traditions, and different again were Caesar's aims in describing the peoples he was fighting in Gaul. Every text is selective. On what bases did the author decide what to include and what to leave out? These are some of the issues we need to confront in dealing with the Greek and Roman texts about the Iron Age Europeans.

Most importantly, we cannot approach the texts as if they were objective statements of fact. As Timpe points out for Roman historical writing, a principal purpose was for the preservation of tradition. Thus in Livy's account of migrations into

Italy and the sack of Rome in the early fourth century BC, for example, we need to consider what aspects of tradition the author was concerned to communicate as he wrote during the time of Augustus. If we can understand the purpose for which an author was writing, then we can better understand the significance and utility of the text.

Texts written about indigenous, non-literate peoples frequently portray them as static, unchanging, passive groups – a theme captured by Eric Wolf in his title *Europe and the People Without History*. For Roman historians during the Republic, Timpe notes that writers had no sense of change among the peoples they described. Even though Caesar mentions migrations and other events that took place before his arrival in Gaul, his portrayal of the Gauls is essentially static. Yet as Chapter 5 shows, the final two centuries BC were times of constant and often profound change.

From our perspective today, it is ironic that Roman writers did not understand the dynamism of the Iron Age peoples, since Roman actions contributed substantially to the changes in the interior of Europe. These actions included the increase in commerce from southern Gaul and northern Italy during the second century BC, the growth of political influence in southern Gaul from the late second century BC and the conquests further northward into the heart of the continent, beginning with Caesar's campaigns in Gaul. Even the processes of observation and inquiry on the part of Roman writers caused change in the ways the indigenous Europeans viewed themselves and others, although this kind of change would be difficult to discern in our present state of understanding. When Caesar asked his informants in Gaul who they were or who their neighbours were, this act inevitably resulted in changes in perception on the part of those asked.

## Inventing the other: Greek and Roman images

Underlying all the specific textual information about peoples and places beyond the Alps lay a strong Greek and Roman idea about the nature of non-Mediterranean peoples and of the landscapes in which they lived. Peoples who did not speak Latin or Greek and did not behave like members of the Mediterranean civilizations were considered barbarians. The term did not have the overly negative connotation that it does today, but referred to people whose way of life was different – simpler and less refined. In judging the meaning of texts about the native peoples of Europe, it is important to bear this essential feature of Greek and Roman perspectives in mind. Even though individual Romans met and worked with individuals from the communities of temperate Europe, there existed this underlying concept that they were different. The texts all present the perspective of highly cultivated, elite Roman men. Non-elites and women are not represented among the authors that wrote about Iron Age Europeans. Roman soldiers and farmers may have thought differently about Europeans they encountered, but no written documents inform us of their perspectives.

Parallel to their attitude to the peoples of the north, Greek and Roman ideas about the lands north of the Alps were that they were wild, uncultivated and dangerous, compared to the familiar, tamed Mediterranean landscape. Textual sources indicate that Romans were aware that the northern lands held considerable resources, but their acquisition was hampered by the difficulties and dangers of the terrain. The written accounts about the peoples and places of the north need to be understood in the context of these basic themes of Greek and Roman thought. To a large extent, the peoples of temperate Europe, as they are represented in the Greek and Roman texts, were invented by the writers, in the same sense that Said has shown that the 'Orient' was largely invented by nineteenth-century European writers and artists, and as Stewart has shown for Roman Britain. Yet the representations were not completely invented – they were based on a reality that was transmitted and transformed by individuals who did not understand the internal workings of the peoples they portrayed.

## Texts and historical traditions

I select three 'events' from the written historical tradition to illustrate the ways that the textual evidence represents historical happenings in Late Iron Age Europe. Several writers mention the migration from northern Europe of peoples they call Cimbri and Teutones, first in the year 113 BC, confronting and defeating a Roman army at Noreia, believed to be in what is now Austria or Slovenia. According to the accounts, these groups, joined during their movements by others, went west into Gaul, then to southern Gaul and eventually into northern Italy, where they were finally defeated by the Roman general Marius at Vercellae, thought to be somewhere in northern Italy, in 101 BC. Although these peoples are commonly referred to in the modern literature as 'Germans,' they were not so designated at the time, nor by Caesar.

The references to movements of the Cimbri and Teutones, and of other groups that migrated in the first half of the first century BC, are complex and ambiguous. The geographical origin of these peoples is unclear. As Lund points out, the common modern linking of the Cimbri with northern Jutland and the Teutones with the southern part of that peninsula has no basis in the ancient sources. Since the archaeological evidence shows that the second and first centuries BC were times of increasingly intensive interaction between peoples all over Europe, we must ask whether the migrations that are mentioned in the ancient sources were just a part of much broader movements, most of which went unnoticed. There is very little material evidence for these migrations as they are described in the texts, either in abandoned landscapes in the north or in the sudden appearance of foreign objects or practices in the areas they are said to have traversed.

Whatever the character of those movements might have been, the descriptions of them by the ancient authors played a significant role in the construction of the Roman view of all peoples beyond the Alps. When Caesar began his campaigning in Gaul in 58 BC, the tradition of the earlier migrations probably played an important role in his thinking about the peoples of Gaul and of the lands across the Rhine. Before Caesar's campaigns, many groups there had been in close contact with Roman Italy and southern Gaul for decades, and some were allies of Rome. Caesar led his army, together with troops from allied Gallic groups and even hired mercenaries whom Caesar called Germans (see below), in conquering those peoples who did not willingly submit to Roman domination. Caesar's commentary provides a relatively detailed account of the year-by-year progress of his campaigns, along with descriptions of some Gallic groups and their way of life. While some of Caesar's technical descriptions are fully supported by the archaeological evidence, notably his description of the *murus Gallicus* fortifications, his accounts of the organization of society and political systems were strongly affected by his Roman perspective.

Caesar's commentary makes clear that much of Gaul must have been in a state of disruption as a result of the war. During the campaigns, his army comprised between 25,000 and 50,000 troops, and much fighting was going on between Gallic groups as well. His armies destroyed villages, burned fields and seized supplies wherever they went. Tens, perhaps hundreds, of thousands of natives died, killed in battle or through starvation or disease in the devastated landscape.

After Caesar's defeat of Vercingetorix and the united Gallic enemies at Alesia in 52 BC, and the putting down of the last remnants of opposition in 51 BC, the conquest of Gaul was complete. Shortly thereafter, Rome began a protracted period of internal discord and civil war, causing a delay in the creation of a provincial infrastructure for Gaul. The textual sources inform us of raids made by groups from east of the Rhine – called Germans – across the river into Gaul. One such raid, in 16 BC, resulted in the defeat of the Fifth Legion under the command of the governor Lollius (Chapter 7). According to the texts, this event caused the emperor Augustus to spend much of the years 15-13 BC in Gaul and on the Rhine frontier organizing defences and establishing forts at Mainz, Bonn, Xanten, Nijmegen and elsewhere and preparing the legions for campaigns across the river into *Germania*. Beginning in 12 BC, Rome established a series of bases on the river Lippe, providing a supply route eastward from the Rhine at Xanten into the German interior.

## Naming the other

All the names of groups in Late Iron Age Europe are known to us from the Greek and Roman texts. In almost all cases, we do not know the origins of these names nor whether the peoples so designated recognized them. As is abundantly illustrated in more recent contexts, names for peoples frequently originate outside of the group. The application of some tribal names to coin legends indicates that some adopted the names by which the Romans designated them, whatever the source of those names may have been. Here I shall highlight three principal problems with the names as they are transmitted in the written sources.

Caesar and other writers designate many different peoples in temperate Europe by name, without explaining the origins of these names or the basis for differentiating between the groups.

Caesar's use of these names to distinguish what he portrays as clearly defined peoples is at odds with the archaeological evidence, which suggests a relatively homogeneous cultural landscape over much of Gaul and across the Rhine. How can these two different pictures of the Iron Age peoples be reconciled?

Greek and Roman authors were inconsistent in their application of names of indigenous peoples. Pohl illustrates the problem with the example of the name Suebi. At one point, Caesar mentions the Suebi as one of many groups represented in the army of Ariovistus. Later, he uses the name in an expanded way. Strabo, writing a few decades after Caesar, uses the name as a collective term that encompasses a number of other named peoples, including Marcomanni, Quadi and Hermunduri. A century later, Tacitus uses the name to designate a larger confederation of peoples. Furthermore, it is not clear whether the name Suebi was originally a self-designator used by a group in temperate Europe, or whether it was created by the Romans.

Roman writers such as Caesar seem not to have been aware that the geopolitical situation in Europe was highly dynamic, that what an individual observed was just a moment in a rapidly-changing cultural environment and that interaction with the Roman world was a major factor in the ongoing changes. Caesar and the other writers portrayed the cultural geography of Gaul and Germany as static until Romans arrived on the scene. Yet as we have seen, the archaeological evidence makes clear that from the beginning of the second century BC, profound changes took place in settlement systems, manufacturing, burial practices and ritual behaviour. The often uncritical reliance of modern investigators on Caesar and other writers has resulted in the adoption of this misunderstanding and has encouraged attempts to trace back into the earlier Iron

Age the very unusual circumstances that the Roman armies encountered north of the Alps.

## Tribalization: process and perception

Neither Caesar nor any other Roman or Greek writer provides the reader with a historical perspective on the tribal groups he names and describes. The archaeology makes clear that the centralized tribal capitals (*civitates* in his words) as Caesar represents the *oppida*, developed only a few decades before Caesar arrived in Gaul. Yet Caesar's portrayal is of an immutable cultural landscape, one that has always been the same. The evidence suggests that the particular formation of communities that Caesar encountered – the tribal groups he designated by names such as Belgae, Helvetii, Sequani, Rauraci and the rest – was a recent phenomenon, and one at least in part caused by interaction with the Roman world. There is no evidence that these groups existed before the intensified Roman activity in southern Gaul during the second century BC.

While the changes were complex, the evidence can be productively understood in terms of the 'tribalization' processes analysed by Ferguson and Whitehead. As Fried notes, the type of society that modern anthropologists categorize as tribal is a common phenomenon on the edges of complex state societies. The salient characteristics of tribes for our purposes here are the existence of a defined tribal territory and the existence of recognized leaders, often of temporary tenure. Ferguson and Whitehead argue that tribes form on the peripheries of complex state societies where previously simpler societies had existed without sharply defined membership, territories or leaders. The principal reason is that state administrators cannot easily deal with the fluid identities, shifting boundaries and alliances and diffuse leadership structures that characterize the majority of indigenous peoples whom they encounter. A tribe, with defined membership, territory and leader, provides the mechanisms states need for effective interaction. Thus agents of expanding states encourage indigenous groups in the creation of tribal structures. This process has been analysed in numerous ethnohistoric contexts worldwide and it provides a useful model for understanding the archaeological evidence from temperate Europe during the second and first centuries BC.

Characteristic in this process is not only the formation of more clearly defined and centralized socio-political groups throughout the central regions of temperate Europe, but also the transformation of many aspects of culture within this 'tribal zone'. The creation of the *oppida* and of the rural farmstead enclosures, the adoption at the centres of new techniques of mass production and the proliferation of coinage often marked with group names are all aspects of processes of centralization and territorial-group identification. The change in funerary practices and development of new behaviours involving deposition of wealth are parts of fundamental changes in ritual and expression that accompanied these transformations in group and territorial identity.

## Celts and Germans

In addition to the tribal names that Caesar, Tacitus and other Roman and Greek writers applied to territorially-distinct groups in Europe, Roman writers drew a distinction between two large, overarching groupings of peoples – Celts, or Gauls, and Germans. These names and Caesar's characterizations of the peoples so designated in the first century BC have played important roles in the thinking of archaeologists and historians about Europeans just before and during the Roman period. These categories continue to play major roles in the ways that many modern national groups perceive themselves and their neighbours (Chapter 1).

From the time of Herodotus, Greek and Roman writers referred to peoples of western and central Europe as Celts or Gauls. Caesar was the first to write extensively about the peoples he called Germans and to distinguish them from Celts. (Posidonius may have discussed them earlier, but his works do not survive.) Caesar presents two principal kinds of information about the Germans.

Germans lived east of the Rhine, while Celts lived west of it, for the most part. In the prevailing Greek cultural-geographical model of Europe to their north, the Celts occupied the lands to the west, the Scythians to the east. In Caesar's portrayal, the Germans inhabited a zone between these two.

The Germans were less civilized than the Celts and thus less like the Romans, and they had a fundamentally simpler way of life. Germans did not live in towns like the *oppida* of Gaul. Their rituals were not as highly developed as those of the Celts, they spent much time hunting and engaged in military activities and they practised little agriculture. In contrast to the Celts of Gaul, the Germans had no permanent leaders and a simpler political system. Caesar asserts (VI.11) that the Celts and Germans comprised different *nationes*. Since the Greek and Roman model of ethnography held that all cultural variables co-varied, Caesar represented these as fundamentally distinct and non-overlapping groups. Yet even in Caesar's account, there are inconsistencies that indicate that the distinction was not as clear-cut as he implies.

Caesar was a military leader composing accounts of his campaigns, and his representations of the peoples in temperate Europe need to be judged in that light. Most historians now agree that the principal purpose of his commentaries was to inform the governing elites of Rome, including members of the senate, of his accomplishments, with an aim to facilitating his accession to greater political power. Much has been written about his motives and his techniques of representation, and these issues need not concern us here. Modern investigators believe that his assertion that the Rhine River formed the border between Celts and Germans was to gain the support he needed to complete his conquest of Gaul. In Greek and Roman cultural geography, rivers were regarded as boundaries between peoples. If, the argument goes, Caesar could convince the political power-holders in Rome that the Rhine was the boundary between one people and another, then when he concluded his campaigns in Gaul, he could claim to have completed the conquest of a people.

Lund's analysis of Caesar's remarks about the Germans provides useful insight into his representation and illustrates some of the complexities involved. In Book II, Caesar distinguishes a small group whom he calls *Germani* who moved from the east of the Rhine across the river into Gaul. In Books IV, V and VI, he uses *Germania* as a geographical term to designate the lands east of the Rhine. He constructs the concept *Germani* – the people who inhabit *Germania* – as a designation for all the peoples east of the Rhine, to create a parallel to the *Galli* west of the Rhine. All the evidence suggests that these names were created by Caesar (or possibly by a predecessor such as Posidonius), not by the indigenous peoples. There is no reason to think that any of the people the Romans called *Germani* at this time thought of themselves as *Germani*, though surely they became aware of Roman usage of that name.

Though Romans as a whole came to accept Caesar's geographical and cultural characterization of the Germans east of the Rhine, and this model of ethnic or cultural division along the Rhine survives in much modern archaeological and historical writing, even in the early Roman Period, Caesar's conception was not accepted by all observers (let alone by the indigenous peoples). The Greek geographer Strabo considered the Germans not as a distinct people, but as part of the larger group known as Celts. And the Greek historian of Rome Cassius

Dio, writing around AD 200, used the geographical term *Keltica* to designate the region that Romans called *Germania*. He used the Latin *Germania* only in the narrow sense of the landscape between the Rhine and the Elbe rivers that Augustus had hoped to annex as a province. Neither the linguistic nor the archaeological evidence supports the distinction that Caesar made between Gauls west of the Rhine and Germans, as a distinct people, east of the river. Neither Caesar nor any other ancient writer used language as a means for distinguishing between Celts and Germans. The linguistic categories 'Celtic' and 'Germanic' are artifacts of scholarly categorization in the nineteenth century, as the field of comparative philology developed, and we should not expect languages that we might identify in Late Iron Age Europe to correspond neatly to those categories.

Nonetheless, inscriptions in Greek and Latin characters on stone, coins and pottery allow linguists to identify certain names and other words that they can link, often tentatively, with languages that are related to the modern categories Celtic and Germanic. In the first century BC, names that can be connected with Celtic occur in western, central and central-eastern Europe; those with Germanic, in central and northern parts of the continent. There is considerable overlap, but Celtic does seem more commonly represented to the west and Germanic to the north. As Meid warns, it is likely that at this time many people spoke languages that would not be easily classifiable into either modern linguistic category, and some that combined elements of both language groups. In days before national borders, textbooks and writing, languages varied much more widely than they do in the modern world.

From the archaeological perspective, the Rhine did not form a cultural boundary during the final centuries of the Iron Age. The *oppida* and the goods produced at them, the rectangular enclosures, metal deposits and other cultural features, were common throughout the landscapes west and east of the river.

East of the *lower* Rhine, on the North European Plain, the situation was different, with smaller-scale societies and less developed economic systems.

If we consider the situation east of the middle and upper Rhine during the period that Caesar was campaigning in Gaul, then we can discern what Caesar may have been writing about when he was describing Germans. Around the time of the Gallic War, many of the *oppida* east of the Rhine declined in activity or were abandoned, people moved out into smaller settlements and the industrial production of pottery, metal and personal ornaments declined (Chapter 5). The evidence in Bavaria of diverse burial practices and small-scale settlements after 60 BC could be interpreted to support the way that Caesar described Germans. After the decline of the *oppida* there, the people indeed had simpler lives than their counterparts in Gaul, the agricultural system was probably in a state of some disarray, and hunting is likely to have become temporarily more important than it had been. With the threat of Roman invasion looming, military preparedness assumed greater importance, as we have seen reflected in the new practice of weapon burial east of the Rhine. In this sense, we can understand Caesar's representing the groups he called Germans, not as a people ethnically distinct from the Gauls, but as groups very like the Gauls whose situation had changed drastically because of his actions.

# 7

# Responding to Representation

In Chapters 2, 3 and 5, I have shown how we can understand changing patterns in the expression of identity in terms of growing mobility in temperate Europe and of increased and more varied interactions between Iron Age Europeans and peoples to the south along the Mediterranean shores and to the north on the North European Plain. Chapters 4 and 6 considered the texts written by Greek and Roman authors that represent the Iron Age peoples through their eyes and their understandings. In this chapter, I examine evidence for some of the ways that peoples of temperate Europe restructured their identities in response to the ways that Romans, in particular, represented them, especially during the final century BC and the first two centuries AD.

In our modern world, we know much about how people respond to the ways they are portrayed by others, and this issue has been both a topic of political concern and the subject of many studies. By the final century BC, many Europeans were involved in a wide variety of interactions with Romans. Commerce, mercenary service and diplomatic meetings were among the arenas of interaction, in the course of which individuals from participating societies gained knowledge and some degree of understanding of the others. In the context of these often regular and intensive interactions, many individuals had ample opportunity to learn how they were regarded by members of the other societies and to restructure their ideas about themselves and their own societies. In this chapter I wish to highlight some of the contexts in which the effects of Roman representations on the identities of people in temperate Europe during these times of intensive interactions can be discerned.

Iron Age Europeans left no written records to tell us how they responded to the ways in which Greeks and Romans represented them, but we can learn much from close scrutiny of the material evidence. In the context of European-native interactions in the Americas, Shoemaker and Krech show how images that European observers created of peoples they called Indians often were adopted and transformed by indigenous peoples in the process of reshaping their identities. In a modern example, native peoples of Tikopia refashioned the ways they viewed themselves on the basis of the representation that an outside observer – an anthropologist – created of them. The processes involved in these changes varied greatly, as they did in Iron Age Europe. In all of these examples, indigenous peoples came to think of themselves, to some extent, the way outsiders thought of and represented them.

I briefly present five examples. Each is complex and merits extensive further investigation.

## Creation of a cavalry elite

The association of spurs and weapons in burials first became common during the first century BC, and that combination was the material expression of a distinctive new identity, that of the horse-riding warrior. In his commentary on the Gallic War, Caesar describes his employment of mercenary cavalry troops, including both Gauls from allied and conquered peoples and Germans from across the Rhine. It is clear from his account that he considered the German cavalry troops especially valuable and that they were accorded considerable honour for their abilities and their loyal service. After Caesar's campaigns in

Gaul, textual sources record German cavalry in Roman military service between 48 and 36 BC in Egypt, north Africa, Macedonia and Sicily.

Spurs occur regularly in the richly outfitted warriors' graves of the second half of that century, on both sides of the Rhine frontier and as far north as central Sweden (Chapter 5), often associated with Roman goods, especially bronze vessels. Sometimes they accompany other horse-related equipment, sometimes they are the only indicator of horse riding. The long swords common in these graves probably were specifically designed as cavalry weapons. In the region around the Moselle River in the western part of the middle Rhineland, spurs are especially common in well-outfitted men's burials, a pattern that might be connected to Caesar's mentioning of the Treveri as particularly good horsemen. The archaeological evidence thus suggests that many of the men who served as cavalry troops with the Roman army, including those from allies in Gaul and individuals from the unconquered lands east of the Rhine, fashioned a new identity based in large part on their roles in the Roman military – in other words, on how Roman generals and soldiers perceived, represented and treated them.

## Rome's 'friendly kings'

On the frontiers of the empire, Rome had a policy of cultivating what are known as 'friendly kings', native potentates who acted as buffers between the imperial lands and potential enemies beyond the frontier. These potentates, some of whom had served as auxiliary leaders with the Roman army, were often granted Roman citizenship, and Rome paid them subsidies in exchange for their protection. These individuals identified both with Rome and with their own societies.

A recently discovered grave at Mušov in Moravia, just north of the Danube frontier, may be that of such a friendly king.

Under a mound of stones and within a spacious wooden chamber were the looted remains of a rich burial that included both Roman and local signs of special status. A complex set of Roman dining ware that included at least eight bronze vessels, silver tableware, glass vessels and ceramic plates implies that the buried individual practised Roman dining customs and connects him with the feasting rituals that played an important role in elite individuals' reaffirmation of their position in their societies. Other special Roman accoutrements included a bronze folding table and a bronze lamp. A set of andirons underscores the significance of feasting. Associated personal ornaments, weapons and sixteen spurs, some ornamented with silver and gold, mark him as a ruler of indigenous character.

This person's identity, as portrayed in the burial, is a complex blending of the role he played in the Roman world and the traditional functions and symbols of the indigenous Iron Age leader. He, or those performing the ceremony that resulted in the construction of the burial assemblage, created this new, complex identity on the basis of the way the Roman world perceived him, integrated into the traditional role of the Iron Age potentate.

## Coin imagery and community identity

During the Late Iron Age, peoples in Europe adopted first Greek and later Roman practice of minting coins with profiled heads on the obverse and meaningful signs on the reverse. In the first century BC, many began including legends written in Latin characters on their coins. In some cases, they were personal names of the minters, in others names of tribes or of places. This practice signals important changes. One is the rise of powerful individuals who led the unifying groups at the time that larger communities formed at the *oppida* (Chapter 5). In part, at least, these changes came about as a result of the ways that Rome dealt with peoples in Europe before the conquest – the way Rome represented them as distinct tribal entities.

In the fashioning of these signs of group identity, the Iron Age communities adopted the Roman medium of coins as political propaganda, with the head of the potentate, often his name and tribally significant imagery on the reverse. A particularly striking case is that of gold coins minted by Vercingetorix. This political unifier and military commander in the final confrontation of Gauls against the Roman army chose to mint coins emblazoned with his name, written in Latin characters around his head, in a fashion similar to that of Roman coins. This form of representation borrows heavily from Roman ideas about the use of coins to convey messages about individual leaders' and group identities, and it shows that Vercingetorix adopted Rome's representation of him and made it his own. This borrowing, by the leader of the final Gallic stand against Roman domination, is ironic.

## Conflict: Roman representation versus indigenous understanding at the Rhine

As explained in Chapter 5, there is no evidence that the River Rhine formed a cultural boundary before Caesar created the eastern border of Gaul at the river, first through his assertions in his commentary that the Rhine formed the border between Celts and Germans, and later through his conquest. What Caesar had said was the cultural or ethnic boundary between two different peoples, he subsequently made the political boundary between conquered Gaul and the unconquered lands east of the Rhine that he called *Germania*. In the decades following the conquest of Gaul, Roman textual sources inform us of incursions by peoples from east of the Rhine across the river into Gaul (Chapter 6). The emperor Augustus spent much of the years 15-13 BC in the Rhineland, overseeing the build-up of defences on the frontier and planning military campaigns into Germanic territory.

Roman texts represent the Germans' incursions as motivated by lust for booty from Roman Gaul, and modern interpretations have tended to accept this portrayal. But in light of discussion in the preceding chapters, a different interpretation might provide a better understanding of these invasions. Rome's establishment of the Rhine as frontier created an artificial boundary through what had been lands inhabited by people who shared a common identity, as far as we can judge from the material evidence (Chapter 5). In creating this frontier, Rome was representing its perception of indigenous peoples' identities as divided at the river, the way Caesar had described them; Rome enforced this representation with military power. But given the archaeological evidence for a high degree of uniformity on the two sides of the Rhine before Caesar's campaigns in Gaul, perhaps the incursions across the Rhine were efforts on the part of unsubdued groups east of the river to challenge Rome's imposition of this frontier. What Roman writers represented as raiding expeditions into Roman territory, the invaders may have viewed as efforts to reunite peoples divided by the foreign enemy.

## Rejecting Romanization: funerary representations as resistance

Roman texts concerning the provinces north of the Alps refer to interactions with the indigenous peoples in terms of pacification and acceptance of Roman ways. Official visual representations, including triumphal arches, relief sculpture and coins, portray subdued and passive natives. But there is abundant evidence, some in texts and much in archaeology, that this official version obscured much that was happening in the provinces. Historically-recorded rebellions make plain that not all native peoples were as submissive as official texts suggest. As Scott shows, most resistance to dominant regimes is not as blatant as rebellion, but takes more subtle forms. In the Roman provinces, varied expressions in funerary ritual challenge the official representations of subdued and docile conquered peoples.

The recently excavated Grave 14 at Goeblingen-Nospelt, situated next to Graves A and B (Chapter 5), included objects characteristic of a woman in Late Iron Age Europe, including eight fibulae and a mirror. Like the others, it contained lavish feasting equipment. Imports from Italy included two bronze basins, a dipper and a sieve and a *terra sigillata* platter from Arezzo. A ceramic amphora held fish sauce. On top of the burial chamber was a ceramic vessel, perhaps for offering libations. Important in relation to continuity of ritual practice was the discovery of small pits in the tumulus containing remains of burned animal bones and, in most cases, a coin that had been in a fire. Altogether 58 coins were recovered in these pits, and they span a period from the penultimate decade BC to the middle of the second century AD. For 150 years, people continued to make offerings at the burial site of this woman. This evidence for repeated offering behaviour focused on this burial monument suggests long-term reaffirmation by those performing the ritual of their identity as people different from Romans.

In southern Bavaria, the graves and water-deposits known as the Heimstetten group embody a different kind of challenge to Roman representation. At the eponymous site of Heimstetten, three inhumation burials contained skeletal remains of women, dating around AD 30-60, accompanied by the kinds of personal ornaments that had characterized Late Iron Age women's graves until the second century BC (Chapter 3) – fibulae, bracelets, glass and amber beads and openwork belt hooks, along with local pottery. Many of the objects are notably archaic in appearance, different from ornaments in common use at the time. The practice of inhumation and the outfitting of these individuals with these categories of ornaments recreates a long-abandoned tradition of funerary ritual, at a time two generations after the Roman conquest of this region in 15 BC. The Heimstetten graves, about 20 of which are known from different parts of southern Bavaria, can be understood as results of community rituals to recreate their identity on the basis of long-remembered funerary traditions, in opposition to Roman-imposed values and practices. Links with past ritual practice are also evident in the water deposits, which involve some of the same kinds of objects as those placed in the burials.

A recently excavated grave at Badenheim in the western Rhineland may illustrate an instance of a community's speaking out against the Roman policy of assimilating indigenous elites into the imperial administrative structure by co-opting them with special status and material paraphernalia of the Roman elite. The grave, from shortly after the middle of the first century BC, contained a sword in an elaborately constructed and ornate scabbard. Most such scabbards accompany graves that are richly outfitted with Roman imported ceramic and bronze vessels. The Badenheim grave, however, contained only seven locally-made pots as additional goods, along with an animal skull, probably from a pig. The lack of Roman products is striking, because virtually all richly outfitted graves in the region from the mid-second century BC on contained Roman vessels, and the special status of the individual is apparent in the presence of the ornate scabbard. The outfitting of this grave and the funerary ceremony that accompanied it may have been performed to communicate the message that this individual and his mourners rejected the Roman idea that local elites would co-operate with the Roman admininstration.

Rejection of Roman-introduced styles and values is apparent in women's burial assemblages and stone sculpture in northern Gaul and the Rhineland, a region from which we have abundant evidence for contention between traditional and introduced

15. Gravestone of Menimane (left) and her husband Blussus, from Mainz-Weisenau, Germany. Note the representation of many aspects of her clothing and personal ornaments, including several different garments, fibulae holding them and a large pendant on her necklace. In contrast, her husband is more plainly attired.

ritual practices. During the first century AD a particular assemblage of dress and personal accoutrements became emblematic of elite women. This set, represented by burials at Nospelt-Krëckelbierg in Luxembourg and Rohrbach in the Saar region of Germany, included four or five fibulae, bronze mirrors, glass perfume bottles and large sets of fine pottery, including imported Roman ceramics. The set of personal clothing attachments marks a distinction from the standard Roman practice, in which women wore metal objects only as ornaments, not as essential components of dress.

The gravestone of a woman named Menimane and her husband Blussus, from Mainz-Weisenau, illustrates the use of this set of fibulae (Figure 15). One fibula holds her tunic-like garment at the front, another an outer garment on her shoulder. A third fibula attaches this wrap to the tunic, and a fourth holds a shawl on the right shoulder. The gravestone is of special significance, beyond showing how the fibulae of this set were worn. The medium – stone sculpture showing individuals, accompanied by a carved Latin text – is Roman. The representation of indigenous dress is a strong statement that the individual felt herself, or those doing the portraying represented her, to be of indigenous character, not Roman. Whether or not she actually wore the kind of clothing portrayed on the sculpture is less important than the choice made for the funerary representation. The similar patterning of fibulae in the burials and on this tombstone indicates that this assemblage of ornaments was a significant sign of the indigenous identity of some women in the century following the Roman conquest of Gaul.

# 8

# Afterthoughts

I argue in this book that we can interpret much of the patterning in the material culture of Iron Age Europe in terms of identity. At the conclusion, I want to pose the question, how can we know whether these interpretations are on the right track? How can we determine whether ornament on Early Iron Age belt plates, walls constructed around settlements, changes in fibula construction in the Late Iron Age and placement of spurs in men's graves really are signs of identity? Can these patterns in the material evidence tell us something about the ways that Iron Age Europeans thought and felt about themselves in relation to others, or are we imposing what we think about identity today upon the archaeological evidence?

These questions go to the root of attempts to understand the human past, in archaeology and in history. As researchers concerned with human behaviour, we cannot avoid imposing our own ideas and experiences on our attempts to evaluate the available data. But by carefully identifying patterns in the material evidence and evaluating them in the context of what we can learn about pre-modern peoples from ethnohistoric situations, I believe that we can develop useful reconstructions that help us to understand, on some level, how people dealt with issues of identity in the past.

By focusing our attention on objects, including personal ornaments, tools and weapons, burial structures and cultural landscapes, that Iron Age people created, rather than relying upon representations of them by others, we have an opportunity to discern people's intentions in the ways they communicated information about themselves. As our understanding of material culture and its relation to communication increases, we should be able to gain greater confidence in the study of this subject.

For the future, I think the most productive possibilities in this line of inquiry lie in the growing emphasis on careful investigation of the contexts, rather than just the contents, of archaeological sites. Instead of focusing primarily on the patterning of postholes on settlements in order to reconstruct houses, or on the character of the objects in rich burials to study social status, we need more of the kind of research that J.D. Hill has conducted on the structured nature of pit deposits on settlements, and that Jörg Biel has carried out at Hochdorf and Otto-Herman Frey and Fritz-Rudolf Herrmann at the Glauberg. Such emphasis on context enables us get closer to human practice in the past – what people actually did and how they did it. But we must rely on analogy – ethnographic and ethnohistoric – to suggest why they did it.

# Bibliographic Essay

The literature on Iron Age Europe, on the Greek and Roman textual sources and on cultural identity is enormous; my citations are selective. In most cases I cite only the most recent work on a topic that will lead the reader to earlier literature, and I cite studies in English whenever possible.

## Preface

Barth 1969 was highly influential in new thinking about identity.

## 1. Identity and the Archaeology of the Iron Age

### Approaching identity in a different world

*Whose view of identity?*
Critical approaches to historical texts: White 1978, Dening 1988. To Greek and Roman texts in particular: Cartledge 1993; Timpe 1989, 1996; Morris 2000. Imperial literature and representations of the other: Pratt 1992, Schwartz 1994.

*Identity and archaeology*
Fundamentally different worlds of others, present and past: Geertz 1983, Lowenthal 1985; specifically for Iron Age: Barrett 1988, Fabech 1991, Hill 1992. Problematic nature of the words we use: Pohl 1997.

*An archaeology of practice*
Differences between non-literate and literate peoples: Goody 2000.

*Ethnicity and identity*
Importance to modern identities of ideas about past peoples: Jones and

Graves-Brown 1996; specific cases: Dietler 1994 on France, Wolfram 1995 on Germany, Schama 1999: 229, 629-38 on Rembrandt; Collis 1996, Evans 1999, James 1999, Megaw and Megaw 1999 on Celts. Venice exhibition: Leclant and Moscati 1991.

*Material culture, identity and agency*
Objects as media of communication: Shanks and Tilley 1987; material evidence as indication of social practice: Barrett 1988; DeMarrais *et al.* 1996. Identity as fluid, contingent: Bentley 1987, Eriksen 1993. Individual agency in archaeology: Carr and Neitzel 1995.

*Definitions and characteristics of identity*
Graves-Brown *et al.* 1996, Jones 1997 and 1999, Anthony 1998, Grahame 1998, Smith 1999.

**Expressing identity**
*Behaviour and identity*
Relationship between material culture and identity: Shennan 1989, Jones 1997, Pohl 1997 and 1998.

*Material manifestations*
Objects as media of social action: Appadurai 1986, Gosden and Marshall 1999. Material culture and identity: Eriksen 1992; clothing: Eicher 1995; pottery: Dietler and Herbich 1998, MacEachern 1998; jewellery: Sørensen 1997; houses: Hingley 1992, Roymans 1996. Burial practice: Pearson 1999. Everyday life as expression of identity: Dening 1988: 99, Linde-Laursen 1993, Jones 1999. Ritual: Rappaport 1999. Materialization: DeMarrais *et al.* 1996.

*Identifying others*
Outsiders' representations: Said 1978, Dening 1988, Hartog 1988, Pratt 1992, Schwartz 1994, Krech 1999.

**Dynamics of identity**
*Change and identity*
Jones 1997: 95 presents examples from Comaroff and Comaroff 1992: 235-63.

*How material culture structures identity*
Material culture structures identity: Csikszentmihalyi and Rochberg-Halton 1981, Appadurai 1986. Imported goods and identity: Helms 1988, Rogers 1990, Thomas 1991, Orlove and Bauer 1997.

*Outsiders' texts and dynamics of identity*
Widespread phenomenon: Hartog 1988. Early Mesopotamia: Nissen and Renger 1987. China: *Tso chuan*, Mesoamerica: *Florentine Codex*. Early modern period: Greenblatt 1991, Pratt 1992, Schwartz 1994. Lack of understanding of indigenous peoples' history: Wolf 1982, Timpe 1996. Raleigh: Whitehead 1997. Identity change in contact-period America: Albers 1996, Hickerson 1996, Hill 1996.

*The 'tribal zone'*
Tribe as category: Fried 1975. Tribalization process: Ferguson and Whitehead 1992, Hill 1996.

*Mobility, interaction and identity*
Long-distance effects of expanding states: Farriss 1984. Contact and political and status identity of leaders: Helms 1988. Roles of imports: Hansen 1995.

## 2. Changing Identities in Early Iron Age Europe

**Concept and character of the Iron Age**
Overviews of Iron Age archaeology: Collis 1984a, Cunliffe 1997.

**New patterns of material expression**
Late Bronze Age: Harding 2000. Belt plaques: Kilian-Dirlmeier 1972 and 1975. Dattingen and Magdalenenberg: Alt *et al.* 1995. Enclosed farmsteads: Nagler-Zanier 1999. Regional groupings in Late Bronze Age: Kristiansen 1998: 64 fig. 26; Early Iron Age: Griesa and Weiss 1999. Elite burial practices in different regions: Pare 1997, Alvarez-Sanchís 2000, Biel 1985a, Dobiat 1980, Egg 1996a, Kull and Stinga 1997, Rolle 1989, Palavestra 1994.

**Mobility and interaction**
Individual mobility in Bronze Age: Jockenhövel 1991. Ilse cemetery:

Bérenger 2000. Witaszkowo: Alexandrescu 1997. Mobility in Eurasia and the Mediterranean: Sherratt and Sherratt 1993, Shanks 1999.

**Interaction and identity**
Distinctive neighbouring communities on middle Elbe: Weiss 1999.

**Imports, elites and regionality**
Hochdorf: Biel 1985a, 1996; Krausse 1999. Feasting remains at kurgans: Onyshkevych 1999. Pits in kurgans: Pshenichniuk 2000. Enclosure and sculptures at Vix: Chaume, Olivier and Reinhard 1995, Chaume 1997. Centres: Alvarez-Sanchís 2000, Chaume 1997, Kimmig 1983, Stična: Gabrovec 1974, Belsk: Rolle 1989, Melyukova 1995.

**Iconography and identity**
Human figure in Early Iron Age: Reichenberger 1995, Bouzek 1997. Strettweg: Egg 1996b. Hirschlanden: Zürn 1970. Greek and steppe iconography: Boardman 1996, Koch 1998, Reeder 1999.

## 3. Creating Interregional Identities

**New style of ornament**
La Tène style: Jacobsthal 1944, Pauli 1978, Megaw and Megaw 1989, Frey 1995a. Steppe art influence: Guggisberg 1998.

**Rich burials and the new style**
Early La Tène rich graves: Verger 1995, Echt 1999. Martial ideology: Roymans 1993. Gündlingen: Dehn 1994. Amulets in Iron Age graves: Pauli 1975. Kurgans of eastern Europe: Melyukova 1995.

**New attitudes toward self and other**
Grafenbühl: Zürn 1970. Grächwil: Frey 1998. Kleinaspergle cups: Böhr 1988, Schaaff 1988. Plzeň-Roudná: Bašta *et al.* 1989. Glauberg: Frey and Herrmann 1997, Herrmann 2000.

**Spread of the La Tène style**
Style spread and identity: Frey 1995b, Megaw and Megaw 1995:346, Fitzpatrick 1996. Early and middle La Tène burials: Lorenz 1978. Iwanowice: Woźniak 1991. La Tène in eastern Europe: Woźniak 1976,

Zirra 1991. Status in middle La Tène cemeteries: Waldhauser 1987. Helmets: Megaw and Megaw 1989.

**Public ritual**

Závist: Motyková *et al.* 1988. Gournay-sur-Aronde: Brunaux 1995, 1996. Duchcov: Motyková 1986. Hjortspring: Kaul 1988. Rogozon: Kull 1997. Filippovka: Pshenichniuk 2000. Change in ritual and society: Fabech 1991.

## 4. Representations of the Other: First Texts

**Context and significance of first naming**

On the name *Keltoi*: Niese 1910: 610-11, Freeman 1996, Cunliffe 1997. *Skythai*: Alekseev 2000. Columbus example: Todorov 1984.

**Greek concepts of ethnicity**

Cartledge 1993, Hall 1997, Romm 1998.

**Texts and migrations**

Syntheses in Rankin 1987 and 1995, Dobesch 1991, Szabó 1991a. Livy: Kraus and Woodman 1997, pp. 51-81. Celts in Italy: Frey 1995b. Mercenaries: Szabó 1991b. Migration as a phenomenon: Anthony 1990 and 1997, Härke 1998. Pictorial representations of Celts: Andreae 1991.

**Who were the Greeks' Celts?**

Chapman 1992, Evans 1999, Megaw and Megaw 1999. Related issue regarding *Skythai*: Alekseev 2000.

## 5. Territoriality and Identity in the Late Iron Age Landscape

**Creating new boundaries**

*Oppida*: Collis 1984b, 1995; Colin 1998. Survey at Kelheim: Murray 1993. Rectangular enclosures: Venclová 1998, Wieland 1999. Bopfingen: Krause and Wieland 1993; Nordheim: Neth 1999. Gournay and Ribemont: Brunaux 1996 and 1999. Fellbach-Schmiden: Planck 1982. Danebury: Cunliffe 1992. Structured deposits: Hill 1995.

**New patterns of deposition**

Change in funerary practice: Krämer 1985, Frey 1986. Skeletal evidence from Manching and other sites: Lange 1983, Hahn 1992, ter Schegget 1999. Kolín and related iron hoards: Rybová and Motyková 1983. Tiefenau: Müller 1990. Llyn Cerrig Bach: Fox 1946. Gold ring and coin hoards: Furger-Gunti 1982. Niederzier: Göbel *et al.* 1991. Wallersdorf: Kellner 1989. Snettisham: Stead 1991. Burned deposit sites: Zanier 1999.

**Material culture and community**

Patterns of manufacturing: Wells 1996. Nauheim fibulae and mass production: Drescher 1955, Furger-Gunti 1977. Gussage All Saints: Foster 1991. Emerging regional political power: Creighton 2000. Coinage: Allen and Nash 1980, Kellner 1990.

**Roman expansion and territorial identity**

Rome's expansion: Dyson 1985, Crawford 1993; in Gaul: Dietler 1997. Expansion of commerce in Mediterranean region after 200 BC: Hopkins 1980. Clemency: Metzler *et al.* 1991. Goeblingen-Nospelt: Metzler 1984. Seine Source and Chamalières: Romeuf 1986. Bolards: Fauduet and Pommeret 1985.

**Interregional identities**

Jastorf: Hässler 1991. Fibula distributions: Völling 1994. New cemeteries in final half first century BC: Rieckhoff 1995, Wells 1995. Weapon burial east of Rhine: Schultze 1986. International warrior elite: Frey 1986, Völling 1992. Harsefeld: Wegewitz 1937. Langå: Albrectsen 1954: 29-30. Gotland: Nylén 1955.

## 6. Outsiders' Views: Roman and Greek Representations

**Accumulating results of entanglements**

Effect of small-scale indigenous societies on larger states: Daunton and Halpern 1999, Wells 1999.

**Texts as cultural constructions**

White 1978 develops this theme. Dening 1988 and Hill 1998 apply it to contact situations. Two perspectives on Ojibway: Bieder 1985. Critical theory in dealing with early texts about others: Sparkes 1997. Issues of representation: Rohatynskyj and Jaarsma 2000. Timpe 1989 and 1996 on Roman texts and European barbarians. Critical analyses of Caesar: Dobesch 1989, Christ 1995. Livy: Kraus and Woodman 1997. Herodotus: Romm 1998. Images of passive natives: Wolf 1982, Shoemaker 1997. Problems of dealing with informants: Clifford 1992. Inquiries by outsiders affect ways people structure, perceive and represent their identities: Whitehead 1997: 63, Wilk 1999.

**Inventing the other**

Greek and Roman ideas about ethnography and cultural geography: Müller 1972, Dauge 1981, von See 1981, Romm 1992, De Caro 1997. Roman ideas about lands and peoples of temperate Europe – Timpe 1989. Construction of the idea of the Orient – Said 1978, Edwards 2000; of Britain in the Roman mind: Stewart 1995.

**Texts and historical traditions**

Cimbri and Teutones: Kaul and Martens 1995, Lund 1998, Pohl 2000. Gallic War: Drinkwater 1983. Augustus in the Rhineland: Heinen 1984.

**Naming the other**

Roman and Greek textual sources: Rankin 1987, Champion 1985, Timpe 1998. Related problems concerning names: Basso 1988, Berkhofer 1988.

**Tribalization**

Chronology of *oppida* in Gaul: Colin 1998. Processes of tribal formation: Ferguson and Whitehead 1992. Examples that bear similarities to the situation of Late Iron Age Europe: Albers 1996, Hill 1996 and 1998, Whitehead 1997.

**Celts and Germans**

I have explored some of these issues in Wells 1995, 1998 and 1999: 99-121. Role of modern identification with these peoples: Graves-Brown *et al.* 1996, James 1998. Roman portrayals of groups known as Germans: Lund 1998, Timpe 1998, Pohl 2000. Linguistic issues: Meid 1986 and Untermann 1989, 1993.

## 7. Responding to Representation

Iron Age peoples learned Romans' ideas about them: Meid 1986:210. Outsiders' representations influence identity construction: Shoemaker 1997, Krech 1999, Macdonald 2000.

**Creation of a cavalry elite**
Spurs as signs of horse-riding warriors in graves: Völling 1992; long swords that characterize these well-outfitted burials: Frey 1986. Gallic and Germanic cavalry in Roman service: Speidel 1994.

**Roman's 'friendly kings'**
Concept of the 'friendly king': Braund 1984. Mušov: Tejral 1992.

**Coin imagery and community identity**
Legends and symbols on Iron Age coins: Allen and Nash 1980, Creighton 2000. Vercingetorix coin: Allen and Nash 1980, numbers 203 and 204.

**Conflict** See Chapter 6.

**Rejecting Romanization**
Example of use of material culture to challenge outsiders' representations: Edwards 2000, Çelik 2000. Rebellions against Rome: Dyson 1975. Subtle forms of resistance: Scott 1990. Goeblingen-Nospelt 14: Metzler 1998. Heimstetten: Keller 1984. Badenheim: Böhme-Schönberger 1998. Indigenous-style dress in Rhineland and northern Gaul: Böhme 1985.

# Works Cited

## Ancient sources

In the text, I refer to works by a number of Greek and Roman writers, including Julius Caesar, Cassius Dio, Herodotus, Livy, Polybius, Strabo and Tacitus. Many English-language editions of these writers' works are available. Especially useful are the Loeb Classical Library editions, published in the United Kingdom by William Heinemann (London) and in the United States by Harvard University Press (Cambridge MA).

## Modern literature


Albers, P.C. 1996. Changing Patterns of Ethnicity in the Northeastern Plains, 1780-1870. In Hill, pp. 90-118.

Albrectsen, E. 1954. *Fynske jernaldergrave*, vol. 1: *Førromersk jernalder*. Copenhagen: Munksgaard.

Alekseev, A. 2000. The Scythians: Asian and European. In Aruz *et al*., pp. 41-8.

Alexandrescu, P. 1997. Zum goldenen Fisch von Witaszkowo (ehem. Vettersfelde). In Becker *et al*., pp. 683-7.

Allen, D.F. and D. Nash. 1980. *The Coins of the Ancient Celts*. Edinburgh: Edinburgh University Press.

Alt, K.W., M. Munz, W. Vach and H. Härke. 1995. Hallstattzeitliche Grabhügel im Spiegel ihrer biologischen und sozialen Strukturen am Beispiel des Hügelgräberfeldes von Dattingen, Kr. Breisgau-Hochschwarzwald. *Germania* 73: 281-316.

Alvarez-Sanchís, J.R. 2000. The Iron Age in Western Spain (800 BC-AD 50). *Oxford Journal of Archaeology* 19: 65-89.

## *Works Cited*

Andreae, B. 1991. The Image of the Celts in Etruscan, Greek and Roman Art. In S. Moscati *et al.*, pp. 61-9.

Anthony, D.W. 1990. Migration in Archaeology. *American Anthropologist* 92: 895-914.

——— 1997. Prehistoric Migration as Social Process. In J. Chapman and H. Hamerow, eds, *Migrations and Invasions in Archaeological Explanation*, pp. 11-20. Oxford: British Archaeological Reports, International Series 664.

——— 1998. Comment on Härke. *Current Anthropology* 39: 26-7.

Appadurai, A. 1986. Commodities and the Politics of Value. In A. Appadurai, ed., *The Social Life of Things*, pp. 3-63. Cambridge: Cambridge University Press.

Aruz, J., A. Farkas, A. Alekseev and E. Korolkova, eds. 2000. *The Golden Deer of Eurasia: Scythian and Sarmatian Treasures from the Russian Steppes*. New York: The Metropolitan Museum of Art.

Barrett, J. 1988. Fields of Discourse: Reconstituting a Social Archaeology. *Critique of Anthropology* 7:5-16.

Barth, F., ed. 1969. *Ethnic Groups and Boundaries*. London: Allen and Unwin.

Basso, K.H. 1988. 'Stalking with Stories': Names, Places, and Moral Narratives among the Western Apache. In E.M. Bruner, ed., *Text, Play, and Story: The Construction and Reconstruction of Self and Society*, pp. 19-55. Prospect Heights IL: Waveland.

Bašta, J., D. Baštová and J. Bouzek. 1989. Die Nachahmung einer attisch rotfiguren Kylix aus Pilsen-Roudná. *Germania* 67: 463-76.

Becker, C., M.-L. Dunkelmann, C. Metzner-Nebelsick, H. Peter-Röcher, M. Roeder, and B. Teržan, eds. 1997. *Beiträge zur prähistorischen Archäologie zwischen Nord- und Südosteuropa*. Espelkamp: Marie Leidorf.

Bentley, G.C. 1987. Ethnicity and Practice. *Comparative Studies in Society and History* 29: 24-55.

Bérenger, D. 2000. Ilse: Ein oberrheinisches 'Ghetto' der frühen Eisenzeit an der Mittelweser? In H.G. Horn, H. Hellenkemper, G. Isenberg and H. Koschik, eds, *Fundort Nordrhein-Westfalen: Millionen Jahre Geschichte*, pp. 247-9. Cologne: Römisch-Germanisches Museum.

Berkhofer, R.F. 1988. White Conceptions of Indians. In W.E. Washburn, ed., *History of Indian-White Relations*, pp. 522-47. Washington: Smithsonian Institution Press.

Bieder, R.E. 1985. Introduction: *Kitchi-Gami: Life Among the Lake Superior Ojibway*, by J.G. Kohl. Trans. L. Wraxall. St. Paul: Minnesota Historical Society Press.

Biel, J. 1985a. *Der Keltenfürst von Hochdorf*. Stuttgart: Konrad Theiss.

——— 1985b. Die Ausstattung des Toten. In D. Planck, J. Biel, G. Süsskind and A. Wais, eds, *Der Keltenfürst von Hochdorf*, pp. 78-105. Stuttgart: Landesdenkmalamt Baden-Württemberg.

——— ed., 1996. *Experiment Hochdorf: Keltische Handwerkskunst Wiederbelebt*. Stuttgart: Keltenmuseum Hochdorf/Enz.

Black, R., W. Gillies and R. O Maolalaigh, eds. 1999. *Celtic Connections*. East Linton, Scotland: Tuckwell Press.

Boardman, J. 1996. *Greek Art*. 4th ed. London: Thames and Hudson.

Böhme, A. 1985. Tracht- und Bestattungssitten in den germanischen Provinzen und der Belgica. In H. Temporini, ed., *Aufstieg und Niedergang der römischen Welt* II, 12, 3, pp. 423-55. Berlin: Walter de Gruyter.

Böhme-Schönberger, A. 1998. Das Grab eines vornehmen Kriegers der Spätlatènezeit aus Badenheim. *Germania* 76: 217-56.

Böhr, E. 1988. Die griechischen Schalen. In Kimmig, pp. 176-90.

Bouzek, J. 1997. *Greece, Anatolia and Europe: Cultural Interrelations during the Early Iron Age*. Jonsered: Paul Astroms Forlag.

Braund, D. 1984. *Rome and the Friendly King*. London: Croom Helm.

Brun, P. and B. Chaume, eds. 1997. *Vix et les éphèmères principautés celtiques*. Paris: Éditions Errance.

Brunaux, J.-L. 1995. Die keltischen Heiligtümer Nordfrankreichs. In Haffner, pp. 55-74.

——— 1996. *Les religions gauloises: Rituels celtiques de la Gaule indépendante.* Paris: Éditions Errance.

——— 1999. Ribemont-sur-Ancre (Somme). *Gallia* 56: 177-283.

Carr, C. and J.E. Neitzel, eds. 1995. *Style, Society, and Person: Archaeological and Ethnological Perspectives*. New York: Plenum.

Cartledge, P. 1993. *The Greeks: A Portrait of Self and Other*. Oxford: Oxford University Press.

Çelik, Z. 2000. Speaking Back to Orientalist Discourse at the World's Columbian Exposition. In Edwards, pp. 77-97.

Champion, T.C. 1985. Written Sources and the Study of the European Iron Age. In T.C. Champion and J.V.S. Megaw, eds, *Settlement and Society: Aspects of West European Prehistory in the First Millennium B.C.*, pp. 9-22. Leicester: Leicester University Press.

Works Cited


Chapman, M. 1992. *The Celts: The Construction of a Myth*. New York: St. Martin's.

Chaume, B. 1997. Vix, Le Mont Lassois: État de nos connaissances sur le site princier et son environnement. In Brun and Chaume, pp. 185-200.

———, L. Olivier and W. Reinhard. 1995. Das keltische Heiligtum von Vix. In Haffner, pp. 43-50.

Christ, K. 1995. Caesar und die Geschichte. In M. Weinmann-Walser, ed., *Historische Interpretationen*, pp. 9-22. Stuttgart: Franz Steiner.

Clifford, J. 1992. Traveling Cultures. In L. Grossberg, C. Nelson and P.A. Treichler, eds, *Cultural Studies*, pp. 96-116. London: Routledge.

Colin, A. 1998. *Chronologie des oppida de la Gaule non méditerranéenne.* Paris: La Maison des Sciences de l'Homme.

Collis, J. 1984a. *The European Iron Age*. London: Batsford.

——— 1984b. *Oppida: Earliest Towns North of the Alps*. Sheffield: Department of Prehistory and Archaeology.

——— 1995. The First Towns. In Green, pp. 159-75.

——— 1996. Celts and Politics. In Graves-Brown *et al.*, pp. 167-78.

Comaroff, J. and J. 1992. *Ethnography and the Historical Imagination*. Boulder: Westview Press.

Crawford, M. 1993. *The Roman Republic*. 2nd ed. Cambridge MA: Harvard University Press.

Creighton, J. 2000. *Coins and Power in Late Iron Age Britain*. Cambridge: Cambridge University Press.

Csikszentmihalyi, M. and E. Rochberg-Halton. 1981. *The Meaning of Things*. Cambridge: Cambridge University Press.

Cunliffe, B. 1992. Pits, Preconceptions and Propitiation in the British Iron Age. *Oxford Journal of Archaeology* 11: 69-83.

——— 1997. *The Ancient Celts.* Oxford: Oxford University Press.

Cüppers, H., ed. 1984. *Trier: Augustusstadt der Treverer*. Mainz: Philipp von Zabern.

Dauge, Y.A. 1981. *Le Barbare: Recherches sur la conception romaine de la barbarie et de la civilisation.* Brussels: Latomus.

Daunton, M. and R. Halpern. 1999. British Identities, Indigenous Peoples and the Empire. In M. Daunton and R. Halpern, eds, *Empire and Others: British Encounters with Indigenous Peoples, 1600-1850*, pp. 1-18. Philadelphia: University of Pennsylvania Press.

De Caro, S. 1997. The Northern Barbarians as Seen by Rome. In *Roman Reflections in Scandinavia,* pp. 25-9. Rome: 'L'Erma' di Bretschneider.

Dehn, R. 1994. Das Grab einer 'besonderen Frau' der Frühlatènezeit von Gündlingen, Stadt Breisach, Kreis Breisgau-Hochschwarzwald. *Archäologische Ausgrabungen in Baden-Württemberg 1994*: 92-4.

DeMarrais, E., L.J. Castillo, and T. Earle. 1996. Ideology, Materialization, and Power Strategies. *Current Anthropology* 37: 15-31.

Dening, G. 1988. *History's Anthropology*. New York: University Press of America.

Dietler, M. 1994. 'Our Ancestors the Gauls': Archaeology, Ethnic Nationalism, and the Manipulation of Celtic Identity in Modern Europe. *American Anthropologist* 96: 584-605.

——— 1997. The Iron Age in Mediterranean France: Colonial Encounters, Entanglements, and Transformations. *Journal of World Prehistory* 11: 269-358.

Dietler, M. and I. Herbich. 1998. *Habitus*, Techniques, Style: An Integrated Approach to the Social Understanding of Material Culture and Boundaries. In Stark, pp. 232-63.

Dobesch, G. 1989. Caesar als Ethnograph. *Wiener Humanistische Blätter* 31:18-51.

——— 1991. Ancient Literary Sources. In Moscati *et al.*, pp. 35-41.

Dobiat, C. 1980. *Das hallstattzeitliche Gräberfeld von Kleinklein und seine Keramik*. Graz: Landesmuseum Joanneum.

Drescher, H. 1955. Die Herstellung von Fibelspiralen. *Germania* 33: 40-9.

Drinkwater, J.F. 1983. *Roman Gaul*. Ithaca NY: Cornell University Press.

Dyson, S.L. 1975. Native Revolt Patterns in the Roman Empire. In H. Temporini, ed., *Aufstieg und Niedergang der römischen Welt* II, 3, pp. 138-75. Berlin: Walter de Gruyter.

——— 1985. *The Creation of the Roman Frontier*. Princeton: Princeton University Press.

Echt, R. 1999. *Das Fürstinnengrab von Reinheim: Studien zur Kulturgeschichte der Früh-La-Tène-Zeit.* Bonn: Rudolf Habelt.

Edwards, H. 2000. A Million and One Nights: Orientalism in America, 1870-1930. In Edwards, pp. 11-57.

——— ed., 2000. *Noble Dreams, Wicked Pleasures: Orientalism in America, 1870-1930.* Princeton: Princeton University Press.

Egg, M. 1996a. Einige Bemerkungen zum hallstattzeitlichen Wagengrab von Somlóvásárhely, Kom. Veszprém in Westungarn. *Jahrbuch des Römisch-Germanischen Zentralmuseums Mainz* 43: 327-53.

——— 1996b. *Das hallstattzeitliche Fürstengrab von Strettweg bei Judenburg in der Obersteiermark*. Mainz: Römisch-Germanisches Zentralmuseum.

Eicher, J.B., ed. 1995. *Dress and Ethnicity*. Oxford: Berg.

Eriksen, T.H. 1992. *Us and Them in Modern Societies*. Oslo: Scandinavian University Press.

——— 1993. *Ethnicity and Nationalism*. London: Pluto Press.

Evans, D.E. 1999. Linguistics and Celtic Ethnogenesis. In Black *et al.*, pp. 1-18.

Fabech, C. 1991. Samfundorganisation religiøse ceremonier og regional variation. In C. Fabech and J. Ringtved, eds, *Samfundorganisation og Regional Variation*, pp. 283-352. Aarhus: Jysk Arkaeologick Selskab.

Farriss, N.M. 1984. *Maya Society under Colonial Rule*. Princeton: Princeton University Press.

Fauduet, I. and C. Pommeret. 1985. Les fibules du sanctuaire des Bolards à Nuits-Saint-Georges (Côte-d'Or). *Revue archéologique de l'Est et du Centre-Est* 36: 61-116.

Ferguson, R.B. and N.L. Whitehead., eds. 1992. *War in the Tribal Zone: Expanding States and Indigenous Warfare.* Sante Fe: School of American Research.

Fitzpatrick, A.P. 1996. 'Celtic' Iron Age Europe: The Theoretical Basis. In Graves-Brown *et al.*, pp. 238-55.

*Florentine Codex*, Book 10: *The People*. Trans. C.E. Dibble and A.J.O. Anderson. Santa Fe: School of American Research, 1961.

Foster, J. 1991. Gussage All Saints. In Moscati *et al.*, p. 608.

Fox, C. 1946. *A Find of the Early Iron Age from Llyn Cerrig Bach, Anglesey*. Cardiff: National Museum of Wales.

Freeman, P.M. 1996. The Earliest Greek Sources on the Celts. *Etudes Celtiques* 32: 11-48.

Frey, O.-H. 1986. Einige Überlegungen zu den Beziehungen zwischen Kelten und Germanen in der Spätlatènezeit. *Marburger Studien zur Vor- und Frühgeschichte* 7: 45-79.

——— 1995a. Das Grab von Waldalgesheim: Eine Stilphase des keltischen Kunsthandwerks. In H.-E. Joachim, ed., *Waldalgesheim:*

*Das Grab einer keltischen Fürstin*, pp. 159-206. Bonn: Rheinisches Landesmuseum.

——— 1995b. The Celts in Italy. In Green, pp. 515-32.

——— 1998. Grächwil. In *Reallexikon der germanischen Altertumskunde* 12: 527-9.

Frey, O.-H. and F.-R. Herrmann. 1997. Ein frühkeltischer Fürstengrabhügel am Glauberg im Wetteraukreis, Hessen. *Germania* 75: 459-550.

Fried, M.H. 1975. *The Notion of Tribe*. Menlo Park CA: Cummings.

Furger-Gunti, A. 1977. Zur Herstellungstechnik der Nauheimer-Fibeln. In *Festschrift Elisabeth Schmid*, pp. 73-84. Basel: Geographisch-Ethnologische Gesellschaft.

——— 1982. Der 'Goldfund von Saint-Louis' bei Basel und ähnliche keltische Schatzfunde. *Zeitschrift für schweizerische Archäologie und Kunstgeschichte* 39:1-47.

Gabrovec, S. 1974. Die Ausgrabungen in Stična und ihre Bedeutung für die südostalpine Hallstattkultur. In B. Chropovsky, ed., *Symposium zu Problemen der jüngeren Hallstattzeit in Mitteleuropa*, pp. 163-87. Bratislava: Verlag der slowakischen Akademie der Wissenschaften.

Geertz, C. 1983. 'From the Native Point of View': On the Nature of Anthropological Understanding. In *Local Knowledge*, pp. 55-70. New York: Basic Books.

Göbel, J., A. Hartmann, H.-E. Joachim and V. Zedelius. 1991. Der spätkeltische Goldschatz von Niederzier. *Bonner Jahrbücher* 191: 27-84.

Goody, J. 2000. *The Power of the Written Tradition*. Washington: Smithsonian Institution Press.

Gosden, C. and Y. Marshall. 1999. The Cultural Biography of Objects. *World Archaeology* 31:169-78.

Grahame, M. 1998. Material Culture and Roman Identity: The Spatial Layout of Pompeian Houses and the Problem of Ethnicity. In R. Laurence and J. Berry, eds, *Cultural Identity in the Roman Empire*, pp. 156-78. London: Routledge.

Graves-Brown, P., S. Jones, and C. Gamble, eds. 1996. *Cultural Identity and Archaeology*. London: Routledge.

Green, M., ed. 1995. *The Celtic World*. London: Routledge.

Greenblatt, S. 1991. *Marvelous Possessions: The Wonder of the New World*. Chicago: University of Chicago Press.

Griesa, I. and R.-M. Weiss. 1999. *Hallstattzeit*. Mainz: Philipp von Zabern.

Guggisberg, M. 1998. 'Zoomorphe Junktur' und 'Inversion': Zum Einfluss des skythischen Tierstils auf die frühe keltische Kunst. *Germania* 76: 549-72.

Haffner, A., ed. 1995. *Heiligtümer und Opferkulte der Kelten*. Stuttgart: Konrad Theiss.

Hahn, E. 1992. Die menschlichen Skelettreste. In F. Maier, U. Geilenbrügge, E. Hahn, H.-J. Köhler and S. Sievers, eds, *Ergebnisse der Ausgrabungen 1984-1987 in Manching*, pp. 214-34. Stuttgart: Franz Steiner.

Hall, J.M. 1997. *Ethnic Identity in Greek Antiquity*. Cambridge: Cambridge University Press.

Hansen, U.L. 1995. *Himlingøje-Seeland-Europa: Ein Gräberfeld der jüngeren römischen Kaiserzeit auf Seeland, seine Bedeutung und internationalen Beziehungen*. Copenhagen: Det Kongelige Nordiske Oldskriftsselskab.

Harding, A.F. 2000. *European Societies in the Bronze Age*. Cambridge: Cambridge University Press.

Härke, H. 1998. Archaeologists and Migration. *Current Anthropology* 39: 19-45.

Hartog, F. 1988. *The Mirror of Herodotus: The Representation of the Other in the Writing of History*. Trans. J. Lloyd. Berkeley: University of California Press.

Hässler, H.-J. 1991. Vorrömische Eisenzeit. In H.-J. Hässler, ed., *Ur- und Frühgeschichte in Niedersachsen*, pp. 193-237. Stuttgart: Konrad Theiss.

Heinen, H. 1984. Augustus in Gallien und die Anfänge des römischen Trier. In Cüppers, pp. 32-47.

Helms, M.W. 1988. *Ulysses' Sail: An Ethnographic Odyssey of Power, Knowledge, and Geographical Distance*. Princeton: Princeton University Press.

Herrmann, F.-R. 2000. *Der Glauberg am Ostrand der Wetterau*. Wiesbaden: Landesamt für Denkmalpflege Hessen.

Hickerson, N.P. 1996. Ethnogenesis in the South Plains: Jumano to Kiowa? In Hill, pp. 70-89.

Hill, Jeremy D. 1992. Can We Recognise a Different European Past? A Contrastive Archaeology of Later Prehistoric Settlements in Southern England. *Journal of European Archaeology* 1: 57-75.

——— 1995. *Ritual and Rubbish in the Iron Age of Wessex: A Study on*

*the Formation of a Specific Archaeological Record*. Oxford: British Archaeological Reports, British Series 242.
Hill, Jonathan D. 1996. Introduction: Ethnogenesis in the Americas, 1492-1992. In Hill, ed. 1996, pp. 1-19.
——— 1998. Violent Encounters: Ethnogenesis and Ethnocide in Long-Term Contact Situations. In J.G. Cusick, ed., *Studies in Culture Contact: Interaction, Culture Change, and Archaeology*, pp. 146-71. Carbondale IL: Center for Archaeological Investigations.
——— ed., 1996. *History, Power, and Identity: Ethnogenesis in the Americas, 1492-1992*. Iowa City: University of Iowa Press.
Hingley, R. 1992. Society in Scotland from 700 BC to AD 200. *Proceedings of the Society of Antiquaries of Scotland* 122: 7-53.
Hopkins, K. 1980. Taxes and Trade in the Roman Empire (200 B.C.-A.D. 400). *Journal of Roman Studies* 70: 101-25.
Jaarsma, S.R. and M.A. Rohatynskyi, eds. 2000. *Ethnographic Artifacts: Challenges to a Reflexive Anthropology*. Honolulu: University of Hawai'i Press.
Jacobsthal, P. 1944. *Early Celtic Art*. Oxford: Clarendon Press.
James, S. 1998. Celts, Politics and Motivation in Archaeology. *Antiquity* 72: 200-9.
——— 1999. *The Atlantic Celts: Ancient People or Modern Invention*? London: British Museum.
Jockenhövel, A. 1991. Räumliche Mobilität von Personen in der mittleren Bronzezeit des westlichen Mitteleuropa. *Germania* 69: 49-62.
Jones, S. 1997. *The Archaeology of Ethnicity*. London: Routledge.
——— 1999. Historical Categories and the Praxis of Identity: The Interpretation of Ethnicity in Historical Archaeology. In P.P.A. Funari, M. Hall and S. Jones, eds, *Historical Archaeology*, pp. 219-32. London: Routledge.
Jones, S. and P. Graves-Brown. 1996. Introduction: Archaeology and Cultural Identity in Europe. In Graves-Brown *et al.*, 1-24.
Kaul, F. 1988. *Da våbnene tav: Hjortspringfundet og dets baggrund*. Copenhagen: National Museum.
Kaul, F. and J. Martens. 1995. Southeast European Influences in the Early Iron Age of Southern Scandinavia. *Acta Archaeologica* 66: 111-61.
Keller, E. 1984. *Die frühkaiserzeitlichen Körpergräber von Heimstetten bei München und die verwandten Funde aus Südbayern*. Munich: C.H. Beck.

Kellner, H.-J. 1989. *Der keltische Münzschatz von Wallersdorf*. Munich: KulturStiftung der Länder.
——— 1990. *Die Münzfunde von Manching und die keltischen Fundmünzen aus Südbayern*. Stuttgart: Franz Steiner.
Kilian-Dirlmeier, I. 1972. *Die hallstattzeitlichen Gürtelbleche und Blechgürtel Mitteleuropas*. Munich: C.H. Beck.
——— 1975. *Gürtelhaken, Gürtelbleche und Blechgürtel der Bronzezeit in Mitteleuropa*. Munich: C.H. Beck.
Kimmig, W. 1983. *Die Heuneburg an der oberen Donau*. 2nd ed. Stuttgart: Konrad Theiss.
——— ed., 1988. *Das Kleinaspergle*. Stuttgart: Konrad Theiss.
Koch, J.K. 1998. Symbol einer neuen Zeit. In A. Müller-Karpe, H. Brandt, H. Jöns, D. Krausse and A. Wigg, eds, *Studien zur Archäologie der Kelten, Römer und Germanen in Mittel- und Westeuropa*, pp. 291-306. Rahden: Marie Leidorf.
Krämer, W. 1985. *Die Grabfunde von Manching und die latènezeitlichen Flachgräber in Südbayern*. Stuttgart: Franz Steiner.
Kraus, C.S. and A.J. Woodman. 1997. *Latin Historians*. Oxford: Oxford University Press.
Krause, R. and G. Wieland. 1993. Eine keltische Viereckschanze bei Bopfingen am Westrand des Rieses. *Germania* 71: 59-112.
Krausse, D. 1999. Der 'Keltenfürst' von Hochdorf: Dorfältester oder Sakralkönig? *Archäologisches Korrespondenzblatt* 29: 339-58.
Krech, S. 1999. *The Ecological Indian*. New York: W.W. Norton.
Kristiansen, K. 1998. *Europe Before History*. Cambridge: Cambridge University Press.
Kull, B. 1997. Orient und Okzident: Aspekte der Datierung und Deutung des Hortes von Rogozon. In Becker *et al.*, pp. 689-709.
Kull, B. and I. Stinga. 1997. Die Siedlung Oprişor bei Turnu Severin (Rumänien) und ihre Bedeutung für die thrakische Kunst. *Germania* 75: 551-84.
Lange, G. 1983. *Die menschlichen Skelettreste aus dem Oppidum von Manching*. Wiesbaden: Franz Steiner.
Leclant, J. and S. Moscati. 1991. Foreword. In Moscati *et al.*, pp. 13-14.
Linde-Laursen, A. 1993. The Nationalization of Trivialities: How Cleaning Becomes an Identity Marker in the Encounter of Swedes and Danes. *Ethnos* 58: 275-93.
Lorenz, H. 1978. Totenbrauchtum und Tracht: Untersuchungen zur regionalen Gliederung in der frühen Latènezeit. *Bericht der Römisch-Germanischen Kommission* 59: 1-380.

Lowenthal, D. 1985. *The Past is a Foreign Country*. Cambridge: Cambridge University Press.

Lund, A.A. 1998. *Die ersten Germanen: Ethnizität und Ethnogenese*. Heidelberg: Universitätsverlag C. Winter.

Macdonald, J. 2000. The Tikopia and 'What Raymond Said'. In Jaarsma and Rohatynskyj, pp. 107-23.

MacEachern 1998. Style, Scale and Cultural Variation: Technological Traditions in the Northern Mandara Mountains. In Stark, pp. 107-31.

Megaw, R. and V. 1989. *Celtic Art*. London: Thames and Hudson.

——— 1995. The Nature and Function of Celtic Art. In Green, pp. 345-75.

——— 1999. Celtic Connections Past and Present. In Black *et al.*, pp. 19-81.

Meid, W. 1986. Hans Kuhns 'Nordwestblock'-Hypothese: Zur Prolematik der 'Völker zwischen Germanen und Kelten'. In H. Beck, ed., *Germanenprobleme in heutiger Sicht*, pp. 183-212. Berlin: Walter de Gruyter.

Melyukova, A.I. 1995. Scythians of Southeastern Europe. In J. Davis-Kimball, V.A. Bashilov, and L.T. Yablonsky, eds, *Nomads of the Eurasian Steppes in the Early Iron Age*, pp. 27-62. Berkeley: Zinat Press.

Metzler, J. 1984. Treverische Reitergräber von Goeblingen-Nospelt. In Cüppers, pp. 87-99.

——— 1998. Goeblingen-Nospelt. In *Reallexikon der germanischen Altertumskunde* 12: 268-76.

Metzler, J., R. Waringo, R. Bis, and N. Metzler-Zens. 1991. *Clemency et les tombes de l'aristocratie en Gaule Belgique*. Luxembourg: Musée National d'Histoire et d'Art.

Morris, I. 2000. *Archaeology and Cultural History*. Oxford: Blackwell.

Moscati, S., O.-H. Frey, V. Kruta, B. Raftery and M. Szabó, eds. 1991. *The Celts*. New York: Rizzoli.

Motyková, K. 1986. Duchcov. In *Reallexikon der germanischen Altertumskunde* 6: 311-15.

Motyková, K., P. Drda and A. Rybová. 1988. Die bauliche Gestalt der Akropolis auf dem Burgwall Závist in der Späthallstatt- und Frühlatènezeit. *Germania* 66: 391-436.

Müller, F. 1990. *Der Massenfund von der Tiefenau bei Bern*. Basel: Schweizerische Gesellschaft für Ur- und Frühgeschichte.

Müller, K.E. 1972. *Geschichte der antiken Ethnographie und ethnologischen Theoriebildung* 1. Wiesbaden: Franz Steiner.

Murray, M.L. 1993. The Landscape Survey, 1990-1991. In P.S. Wells, ed., *Settlement, Economy, and Cultural Change at the End of the European Iron Age: Excavations at Kelheim in Bavaria, 1987-1991*, pp. 96-134. Ann Arbor: International Monographs in Prehistory.

Nagler-Zanier, C. 1999. *Die hallstattzeitliche Siedlung mit Grabeneinlage von Geiselhöring, Niederbayern*. Büchenbach: Dr. Faustus.

Niese, B. 1910. Galli. In G. Wissowa and W. Kroll., eds, *Paulys Realencyclopädie der classischen Altertumswissenschaft* 7, 1: 610-39. Stuttgart: Alfred Druckenmüller.

Neth, A. 1999. Zum Fortgang der Ausgrabungen in der zweiten Viereckschanze bei Nordheim, Kreis Heilbronn. *Archäologische Ausgrabungen in Baden-Württemberg 1999*: 75-9.

Nissen, H.-J. and J. Renger, eds. 1987. *Mesopotamien und seine Nachbarn*. Berlin: D. Reimer.

Nylén, E. 1955. *Die vorrömische Eisenzeit Gotlands*. Uppsala: Almqvist & Wiksells.

Onyshkevych, L. 1999. Scythia and the Scythians. In Reeder, pp. 23-35.

Orlove, B. and A.J. Bauer. 1997. Giving Importance to Imports. In B. Orlove, ed., *The Allure of the Foreign: Imported Goods in Postcolonial Latin America*, pp. 1-30. Ann Arbor: University of Michigan Press.

Palavestra, A. 1994. Prehistoric Trade and a Cultural Model for Princely Tombs in the Central Balkans. In K. Kristiansen and J. Jensen, eds, *Europe in the First Millennium B.C.*, pp. 45-56. Sheffield: J.R. Collis Publications.

Pare, C. 1997. La dimension européenne du commerce grec à la fin de la période archaïque et pendant de début de la période classique. In Brun and Chaume, pp. 261-86.

Pauli, L. 1975. *Keltische Volksglaube*. Munich: C.H. Beck.

——— 1978. *Der Dürrnberg bei Hallein III*. Munich: C.H. Beck.

Pearson, M.P. 1999. *The Archaeology of Death and Burial*. College Station: Texas A&M University Press.

Planck, D. 1982. Eine neuentdeckte keltische Viereckschanze in Fellbach-Schmiden, Rems-Murr-Kreis. *Germania* 60: 125-72.

Pohl, W. 1997. Ethnic Names and Identities in the British Isles. In J. Hines, ed., *The Anglo-Saxons from the Migration Period to the*

*Eighth Century: An Ethnographic Perspective,* pp. 7-32. Woodbridge: Boydell Press.

——— 1998. Telling the Difference: Signs of Ethnic Identity. In W. Pohl, ed., *Strategies of Distinction: The Construction of Ethnic Communities, 300-800*, pp. 17-69. Leiden: Brill.

——— 2000. *Die Germanen*. Munich: R. Oldenbourg.

Pratt, M.L. 1992. *Imperial Eyes: Travel Writing and Transculturation*. London: Routledge.

Pshenichniuk, A. 2000. The Filippovka Kurgans at the Heart of the Eurasian Steppes. In Aruz *et al*., pp. 21-30.

Rankin, D. 1987. *Celts and the Classical World*. London: Croom Helm.

——— 1995. The Celts Through Classical Eyes. In Green, pp. 21-33.

Rappaport, R.A. 1999. *Ritual and Religion in the Making of Humanity*. Cambridge: Cambridge University Press.

Reeder, E.D. 1999. Scythian Art. In Reeder, pp. 37-58.

——— ed. 1999. *Scythian Gold: Treasures from Ancient Ukraine*. New York: Harry N. Abrams.

Reichenberger, A. 1995. Figürliche Kunst: Hallstattzeit. In *Reallexikon der germanischen Altertumskunde* 9: 13-20.

Rieckhoff, S. 1995. *Süddeutschland im Spannungsfeld von Kelten, Germanen und Römern*. Trier: Rheinisches Landesmuseum.

Rogers, J.D. 1990. *Objects of Change: The Archaeology and History of Arikara Contact with Europeans*. Washington: Smithsonian Institution Press.

Rohatynskyj, M.A. and S.R. Jaarsma. 2000. Ethnographic Artifacts. In Jaarsma and Rohatynskyi, pp. 1-17.

Rolle, R. 1989. *The World of the Scythians*. Trans. G. Walls. London: Batsford.

Romeuf, A.-M. 1986. Ex-voto en bois de Chamalières (Puy-de-Dôme) et des sources de la Seine. *Gallia* 44: 65-89.

Romm, J.S. 1992. *The Edges of the Earth in Ancient Thought*. Princeton: Princeton University Press.

——— 1998. *Herodotus*. New Haven: Yale University Press.

Roymans, N. 1993. Romanisation and the Transformation of a Martial Elite-Ideology in a Frontier Province. In P. Brun, S. van der Leeuw and C.R. Whittaker, eds, *Frontières d'empire: Nature et signification des frontières romaines*, pp. 33-50. Nemours: Mémoires du Musée de Préhistoire d'Ile-de-France.

——— 1996. The Sword and the Plough: Regional Dynamics in the Romanisation of Belgic Gaul and the Rhineland Area. In N. Roymans, ed., *From the Sword to the Plough*, pp. 9-126. Amsterdam: Amsterdam University Press.

Rybová, A. and K. Motyková. 1983. Der Eisendepotfund der Latènezeit von Kolín. *Památky Archeologické* 74: 96-174.

Said, E.W. 1978. *Orientalism*. New York: Pantheon.

Schaaff, U. 1988. Zu den antiken Reparaturen der griechischen Schalen. In Kimmig, pp. 191-5.

Schama, S. 1999. *Rembrandt's Eyes*. New York: Alfred A. Knopf.

ter Schegget, M.E. 1999. Late Iron Age Human Skeleton Remains from the River Meuse at Kessel: A Cult Place? In F. Theuws and N. Roymans, eds, *Land and Ancestors: Cultural Dynamics in the Urnfield Period and the Middle Ages in the Southern Netherlands*, pp. 199-240. Amsterdam: Amsterdam University Press.

Schultze, E. 1986. Zur Verbreitung von Waffenbeigaben bei den germanischen Stämmen um den Beginn unserer Zeitrechnung. *Jahrbuch der Bodendenkmalpflege in Mecklenburg 1986*: 93-117.

Schwartz, S.B., ed. 1994. *Implicit Understandings: Observing, Reporting, and Reflecting on the Encounters Between Europeans and Other Peoples in the Early Modern Era*. Cambridge: Cambridge University Press.

Scott, J.C. 1990. *Domination and the Arts of Resistance*. New Haven: Yale University Press.

von See, K. 1981. Der Germane als Barbar. *Jahrbuch für Internationale Germanistik* 13: 42-72.

Shanks, M. 1999. *Art and the Greek City State*. Cambridge: Cambridge University Press.

Shanks, M. and C. Tilley. 1987. *Social Theory and Archaeology*. London: Polity Press.

Shennan, S., ed. 1989. *Archaeological Approaches to Cultural Identity*. London: Unwin Hyman.

Sherratt, S. and A. 1993. The Growth of the Mediterranean Economy in the Early First Millennium BC. *World Archaeology* 24: 361-78.

Shoemaker, N. 1997. How Indians Got to be Red. *American Historical Review* 102: 625-44.

Smith, A.D. 1999. *Myths and Memories of the Nation*. Oxford: Oxford University Press.

Sørensen, M.L.S. 1997. Reading Dress: The Construction of Social Categories and Identities in Bronze Age Europe. *Journal of European Archaeology* 5: 93-114.

Sparkes, B.A. 1997. Some Greek Images of Others. In B. Molyneaux, ed., *The Cultural Life of Images*, pp. 130-57. London: Routledge.
Speidel, M.P. 1994. *Riding for Caesar: The Roman Emperors' Horse Guards*. Cambridge MA: Harvard University Press.
Stark, M.T., ed. 1998. *The Archaeology of Social Boundaries*. Washington: Smithsonian Institution Press.
Stead, I.M. 1991. The Snettisham Treasure. *Antiquity* 65: 447-64.
Stewart, P.C.N. 1995. Inventing Britain: The Roman Creation and Adaptation of an Image. *Britannia* 26: 1-10.
Szabó, M. 1991a. The Celts and Their Movements in the Third Century B.C. In Moscati *et al.*, pp. 303-19.
——— 1991b. Mercenary Activity. In Moscati *et al.*, pp. 333-6.
Tejral, J. 1992. Die Probleme der römisch-germanischen Beziehungen unter Berücksichtigung der neuen Forschungsergebnisse im niederösterreichisch-südmährischen Thayaflussgebiet. *Bericht der Römisch-Germanischen Kommission* 73: 377-468.
Thomas, N. 1991. *Entangled Objects: Exchange, Material Culture, and Colonialism in the Pacific*. Cambridge MA: Harvard University Press.
Timpe, D. 1989. Entdeckungsgeschichte: Die Römer und der Norden. *Reallexikon der germanischen Altertumskunde* 7: 337-47.
——— 1996. *Memoria* und Geschichtsschreibung bei den Römern. In H.-J. Gehrke and A. Möller, eds, *Vergangenheit und Lebenswelt*, pp. 277-99. Tübingen: Gunter Narr Verlag.
——— 1998. Germanen: historisch. *Reallexikon der germanischen Altertumskunde* 11: 182-245.
Todorov, T. 1984. *The Conquest of America: The Question of the Other*. Trans. R. Howard. New York: Harper and Row.
*The Tso chuan: Selections from China's Oldest Narrative History*. Trans. B. Watson. New York: Columbia University Press, 1989.
Untermann, J. 1989. Sprachvergleichung und Sprachidentität: Methodische Fragen im Zwischenfeld von Keltisch und Germanisch. In H. Beck., ed., *Germanische Rest- und Trümmersprachen*, pp. 211-39. Berlin: Walter de Gruyter.
——— 1993. Sprachliche Zeugnisse der Kelten in Süddeutschland. In H. Dannheimer and R. Gebhard, eds, *Das keltische Jahrtausend*, pp. 23-7. Mainz: Philipp von Zabern.
Venclová, N. 1998. *Mšecké Žehrovice in Bohemia: Archaeological Background to a Celtic Hero, 3rd-2nd Cent. B.C.* Sceaux: Kronos.

Verger, S. 1995. De Vix à Weiskirchen: La transformation des rites funéraires aristocratiques en Gaule du nord et de l'est au Ve siècle avant J.-C. *Mélanges de l'École française de Rome, Antiquité* 107: 335-458.

Völling, T. 1992. Dreikreisplattensporen. *Archäologisches Korrespondenzblatt* 22: 393-402.

——— 1994. Studien zu Fibelformen der jüngeren vorrömischen Eisenzeit und ältesten römischen Kaiserzeit. *Bericht der Römisch-Germanischen Kommission* 75:147-282.

Waldhauser, J. 1987. Keltische Gräberfelder in Böhmen. *Bericht der Römisch-Germanischen Kommission* 68: 25-179.

Wegewitz, W. 1937. *Die langobardische Kultur im Gau Moswidi (Niederelbe)*. Hildesheim: August Lax.

Weiss, R.M. 1999. Die Hallstattzeit in Europa. In Griesa and Weiss, pp. 7-22.

Wells, P.S. 1995. Identities, Material Culture, and Change: 'Celts' and 'Germans' in Late-Iron-Age Europe. *Journal of European Archaeology* 3:169-85.

——— 1996. Location, Organization, and Specialization of Craft Production in Late Prehistoric Central Europe. In B. Wailes, ed., *Craft Specialization and Social Evolution*, pp. 85-98. Philadelphia: University Museum.

——— 1998. Identity and Material Culture in the Later Prehistory of Central Europe. *Journal of Archaeological Research* 6: 239-98.

——— 1999. *The Barbarians Speak: How the Conquered Peoples Shaped Roman Europe*. Princeton: Princeton University Press.

White, H. 1978. The Historical Text as Literary Artifact. In *Tropics of Discourse: Essays in Cultural Criticism*, pp. 81-100. Baltimore: Johns Hopkins University Press.

Whitehead, N.L. 1997. Transcription, Annotation, and Introduction of Walter Ralegh, *The Discoverie of the Large, Rich, and Bewtiful Empyre of Guiana*. Norman: University of Oklahoma Press.

Wieland, G., ed. 1999. *Keltische Viereckschanzen*. Stuttgart: Konrad Theiss.

Wilk, R.R. 1999. 'Real Belizean Food': Building Local Identity in the Transnational Caribbean. *American Anthropologist* 101: 244-55.

Wolf, E.R. 1982. *Europe and the People Without History*. Berkeley: University of California Press.

Wolfram, H. 1995. *Die Germanen*. 2nd ed. Munich: C.H. Beck.

Woźniak, Z. 1976. Die östliche Randzone der Latènekultur. *Germania* 54: 382-402.

——— 1991. The Iwanowice Cemetery. In Moscati *et al.*, p. 378.

Zanier, W. 1999. *Der spätlatènezeitliche und römerzeitliche Brandopferplatz im Forggensee (Gde. Schwangau).* Munich: C.H. Beck.

Zirra, V.V. 1991. Entre l'utile et l'art: les fibules latèniennes en Roumanie. *Etudes Celtiques* 28: 451-64.

Zürn, H. 1970. *Hallstattforschungen in Nordwürttemberg*. Stuttgart: Staatliches Amt für Denkmalpflege.

# Index

The names Celts, Germans, Greeks, Romans and Scythians, and the words burial, ethnicity, identity, material culture and text occur throughout the book and are not indexed.

VERMONT STATE COLLEGES
0 0003 04162605